COOL
Barcelona

teNeues

Imprint

Editors: Martin Nicholas Kunz, Editorial coordination: Mariel Marohn

Photos (location): all photos Xavier Babarro, beside: © Au nom de la rose (Au nom de la rose), © Blow (Blow by Le Swing), © Derby Hotels (GBar, p. 4 b.l.), © Drolma Restaurant (Drolma Restaurant), © Elephant (Elephant), © Els Pescadors (Els Pescadors), Michelle Galindo (Platja de la Barceloneta p. 193 and Transbordador Aeri del Port p. 209), © Grup 7 Portes (Flash Flash Tortilleria and Il Giardinetto), © Grupo Tragaluz (Tragaluz p. 69, Cuines Santa Caterina p.34), Francisco Guerrero (Angels & Kings, p. 10), © hoss intropia (hoss intropia, p. 8 b.l.), Martin Nicholas Kunz (El Japonés, Negro, Tragaluz p.70, 71), © LA FOTOGRAFICA (Casa Munich, p. 4 b.r.), © Lotus Theater (Lotus Theater), Rebecca McNally Coleman and Jose Hernandez Rojas (Milk), Carlos Allende Mèlich, Studio 75 (Nobodinoz), © Oriol Balaguer (Oriol Balaguer), © Otto Zutz (Otto Zutz), Jose Hernandez Rojas (Marmalade), © Vinçon Barcelona (Vinçon, p. 11 b.r.)

Cover photo (location): © Vinçon Barcelona (Vinçon)

Back cover photos from top to bottom (location): Xavier Babarro (Cuines Santa Caterina, CDLC, Comerç24, Gran Teatre del Liceu)

Price categories: € = reasonable, €€ = moderate, €€€ = upscale, €€€€ = expensive

Introduction, texts: Jutta Vey

Layout & pre-press, imaging: fusion publishing

Translations: Zoratti studio editoriale: Lizzie Gilbert (English), Laurence Lenglet (French), Virtudes Mayayo (Spanish)

Produced by fusion publishing GmbH, Berlin   www.fusion-publishing.com

Published by teNeues Publishing Group

teNeues Verlag GmbH + Co. KG
Am Selder 37
47906 Kempen, Germany
Tel.: 0049-(0)2152-916-0
Fax: 0049-(0)2152-916-111
E-mail: books@teneues.de

Press department:
arehn@teneues.de
Tel.: 0049-2152-916-202

www.teneues.com

ISBN: 978-3-8327-9202-2

© 2009 teNeues Verlag GmbH + Co. KG, Kempen

Printed in China

teNeues Publishing Company
16 West 22nd Street
New York, NY 10010, USA
Tel.: 001-212-627-9090
Fax: 001-212-627-9511

teNeues Publishing UK Ltd.
York Villa, York Road
Byfleet
KT14 7HX, Great Britain
Tel.: 0044-1932-403509
Fax: 0044-1932-403514

teNeues France S.A.R.L.
93, rue Bannier
45000 Orléans, France
Tel.: 0033-2-38541071
Fax: 0033-2-38625340

Bibliographic information published by the Deutsche Nationalbibliothek.

The Deutsche Nationalbibliothek lists this publication in the Deutsche Nationalbibliografie; detailed bibliographic data are available in the Internet at http://dnb.d-nb.de.

RESTAURANTS & CAFÉS

CLUBS, LOUNGES & BARS

SHOPS

HIGHLIGHTS

SERVICE

Introduction

More than two thousand years old and still crazy—this city rocks! Ancient yet exhilaratingly young, unchanged yet extremely hip, romantic yet avant-garde—that's Barcelona. It's no wonder that the seaport is also called "Europe's New York."

The Barri Gòtic, one of Europe's best preserved medieval quarters, oozes history at every turn—yet it has got its finger right on the pulse with its many innovative shops and stylish bars. Apropos style: awesome yet playful modernist architecture such as Antoni Gaudí's unfinished cathedral Sagrada Família and audacious postmodern glass constructions such as the Torre Agbar give the city its unmistakable, charismatic feel.

Imagination provides the *je ne sais quoi*—the same can be said for eating and drinking in Barcelona. Countless creative chefs improve the traditionally savory Catalan cuisine in such an ingenious way that the Mediterranean metropolis has long become a hotspot for gourmets. And another thing: Barcelona is the city with the highest number of bars, taverns and discos per capita in the world. Revelers of all persuasions get their money's worth as the club scene belongs to Europe's most innovative. Add to that an El Dorado for fans of architecture, gourmets, shopaholics, and socialites. What else? Sunbathing, swimming, surfing on the three-mile long beach! Enigmatic, trendy, hot—this city never sleeps. *Viva la vida*!

Jutta Vey

Einleitung

Über zweitausend Jahre und kein bisschen leise – diese Stadt rockt! Uralt und prickelnd jung, ursprünglich und extrem hip, romantisch und avantgardistisch – all das ist Barcelona. Kein Wunder, dass die Hafenstadt auch „das New York Europas" genannt wird.

Im Barri Gòtic, einem der besterhaltenen mittelalterlichen Stadtviertel Europas, atmet man auf Schritt und Tritt Geschichte – und ist zugleich immer am Puls der Zeit, finden sich hier doch auch viele innovative Shops und stylische Bars. Apropos Style: Prächtige verspielte Modernisme-Bauten wie Antoni Gaudís unvollendete Kathedrale Sagrada Família und kühne postmoderne Glasarchitektur wie der Torre Agbar geben der Stadt ihr unverwechselbares, charismatisches Gesicht.

Genie durch Phantasie – das gilt auch für die gastronomische Szene Barcelonas. Unzählige kreative Küchenchefs verfeinern in ihren Restaurants die traditionell herzhafte katalanische Küche so virtuos, dass die Mittelmeermetropole unter Feinschmeckern längst ein absoluter Hotspot ist. Darüber hinaus ist Barcelona weltweit die Stadt mit der höchsten Anzahl an Bars, Kneipen und Diskotheken pro Einwohner. Hier kommen Nachtschwärmer aller Couleur auf ihre Kosten, die Clubszene gehört zu den innovativsten Europas. Eldorado für Architekturfans, Gourmets, Shopaholics, Partygänger. Und was noch? Sonnen, Schwimmen und Surfen am fünf Kilometer langen Strand! Schillernd, trendy, quicklebendig – diese Stadt schläft nie. Viva la vida!

Jutta Vey

Introduction

Avec ses deux mille ans d'histoire et son grain de folie, cette ville nous bouscule ! A la fois hors d'âge et incroyablement jeune, immuable et extrêmement branchée, romantique et avant-gardiste – voici Barcelone. On ne s'étonnera donc pas que cette ville portuaire soit souvent comparé à New York.

Le Barri Gòtic, l'un des quartiers médiévaux les mieux préservés en Europe, est à chaque coin de rue un véritable concentré d'histoire, mais avec ses boutiques tendance et ses bars chics, il a su rester en prise avec le rythme trépidant de la vie d'aujourd'hui. A propos d'innovation, la Sagrada Família, cathédrale inachevée, aussi impressionnante que ludique, de l'architecte moderniste Antonio Gaudí, et la Torre Agbar, audacieuse structure de verre postmoderne, confèrent à cette ville un charisme inimitable.

L'imagination et le génie sont aussi au rendez-vous dans les restaurants et les bars de Barcelone. Les chefs rivalisent ici de créativité pour revisiter la savoureuse cuisine traditionnelle catalane, à tel point que la métropole méditerranéenne s'est imposée comme une véritable plaque tournante de la gastronomie. Autre chose : Barcelone détient le record du monde en matière de nombre de bars, de tavernes et de boîtes de nuit par habitant. Les noctambules en tout genre en auront ici pour leur argent car la scène barcelonaise est l'une des plus innovantes d'Europe. Paradis des passionnés d'architecture, des gourmets, des accros du shopping et des fêtards… Quoi d'autre ? Une plage de cinq kilomètres, paradis des nageurs, des surfeurs et des inconditionnels du bronzage. Enigmatique, branchée, incontournable, c'est une ville qui ne dort jamais. Viva la vida !

Jutta Vey

Introducción

Más de dos mil años y tanta fuerza: ¡esta ciudad es trepidante! Milenaria y superlativamente joven, genuina y en extremo moderna, romántica y vanguardista: todo eso es Barcelona. No resulta extraño que algunos llamen a esta ciudad portuaria "la Nueva York europea". En el Barri Gòtic, uno de los barrios medievales mejor conservados de Europa, se respira historia paso a paso y, a la vez, se está siempre a la última, pues en sus calles se han establecido también buen número de comercios innovadores y bares de diseño. A propósito de diseño: las líneas juguetonas de obras modernistas espléndidas, como la incompleta catedral de la Sagrada Família, de Antoni Gaudí, y una audaz arquitectura posmoderna con recubrimientos en vidrio, como la Torre Agbar, confieren a la ciudad un rostro inconfundible y carismático.

Por la vía de la fantasía, a la genialidad: algo que también es válido para el escenario gastronómico barcelonés. Innumerables chefs de cocina de gran creatividad han refinado en sus restaurantes la suculenta cocina tradicional catalana con tal virtuosismo que han convertido a esta metrópoli mediterránea en una estación obligatoria para los paladares más selectos. Además, Barcelona es la ciudad internacional que cuenta con mayor número de bares, tascas y discotecas por habitante. Noctámbulos de todos los gustos y colores se sienten en Barcelona en su salsa, el ambiente de sus clubes nocturnos es uno de los más pujantes de Europa. El dorado de los fans de la arquitectura y de la buena comida, de los adictos a las compras y a las fiestas. ¿Y algo más? Además se puede tomar el sol, nadar o hacer surf en sus cinco quilómetros de playa. Chispeante, moderna, vibrante: esta ciudad nunca duerme. ¡Viva la vida!

Jutta Vey

RESTAURANTS & CAFÉS

Casa Calvet

Carrer de Casp, 48
08010 Barcelona
Eixample
Phone: +34 / 93 / 4 12 40 12
www.casacalvet.es

Opening hours: Mon–Fri 1 pm to 3.30 pm and 8.30 pm to 11 pm, closed on Sun and legal holidays
Prices: €€€
Cuisine: Mediterranean
Public transportation: Metro Urquinaona
Map: No. 1

A former office block turned into a gourmet's paradise: the art nouveau Casa Calvet, the only building for which architect Antoni Gaudí received an award during his lifetime, has been home to fine restaurants since 1994. Chef Miquel Alija refines Catalan cuisine with an Asian finesse. Be it partridge with chestnuts or rosemary ice cream for dessert—the menu will surprise even discerning connoisseurs.

Früher Bürohaus, heute Gourmet-Tempel: In der Casa Calvet, dem einzigen Gebäude, für das der Architekt Antoni Gaudí zu Lebzeiten eine offizielle Auszeichnung erhielt, kann man seit 1994 in schickem Jugendstilambiente erlesen speisen. Restaurantchef Miquel Alija veredelt die katalanische Küche mit asiatischer Raffinesse. Ob Rebhuhn mit Kastanien oder Rosmarineis zum Dessert – die Speisekarte überrascht auch anspruchsvolle Genießer.

Jadis immeuble de bureaux de style art nouveau, aujourd'hui temple des gourmets, la Casa Calvet, seule réalisation pour laquelle Antonio Gaudí fut primé de son vivant, propose, depuis 1994, une table de qualité. Ici, le chef Miquel Alija marie la cuisine catalane au raffinement asiatique. Perdrix aux marrons, glace au romarin en dessert : la carte surprendra les plus fins connaisseurs.

De inmueble de oficinas a templo para *gourmets*: en la Casa Calvet, el único edificio por el que su arquitecto, Antoni Gaudí, recibió un premio oficial en vida, se puede disfrutar desde 1994 de una comida selecta en un elegante ambiente modernista. El chef del restaurante, Miquel Alija, enriquece la cocina catalana con la sutileza asiática. Ya sea perdiz con castañas o helado de romero de postre, la carta sorprende incluso a los sibaritas más exigentes.

CheeseMe

Plaça Jacint Reventós s/n (opposite Calle Argentería, 53)
08003 Barcelona
Ciutat Vella
Phone: +34 / 93 / 2 68 11 27
www.cheeseme.org

Opening hours: Mon–Sun noon to 2 am
Prices: €€
Cuisine: Cheese dishes, nouvelle cuisine, tapas
Public transportation: Metro, bus Jaume I
Map: No. 2

Cheese in all its forms plays the main role in this restaurant—from starter to dessert. To name a few of the house's specialties: Manchego lasagna with anchovies or artisan homemade cheesecake with vanilla ice cream as a dessert. The menu also boasts a section called "Antiquesos"—cheese-free alternatives. The original design is by architect Jonathan Daifuku.

In diesem Restaurant spielt von der Vorspeise bis zum Dessert Käse in all seinen Variationen die Hauptrolle. Zu den Spezialitäten des Hauses gehören die Manchego-Lasagne mit Anchovis sowie selbstgemachter Käsekuchen mit Vanilleeis. Die Karte bietet unter „Antiquesos" aber auch einige „käsefreie" Alternativen. Das originelle Design stammt von Architekt Jonathan Daifuku.

De l'entrée au dessert, le fromage sous toutes ses formes tient ici le rôle principal. Parmi les spécialités maison, on peut citer les lasagnes au manchego et aux anchois, et, en dessert, le gâteau au fromage blanc artisanal avec une boule de glace à la vanille en dessert. Mais la carte tient compte également des Antiquesos (« anti-fromage ») en proposant une sélection de plats d'où le fromage est absent. La décoration intérieure est signée Jonathan Daifuku.

En este restaurante, el queso, en todas sus variaciones, es el protagonista desde los entrantes hasta el postre. Entre las especialidades de la casa se cuentan la lasaña de manchego con anchoas o el pastel de queso con helado de vainilla. En el apartado "Antiquesos", la carta ofrece también algunas alternativas sin queso. Su original diseño es obra del arquitecto Jonathan Daifuku.

Comerç24

Carrer del Comerç, 24
08003 Barcelona
Ciutat Vella
Phone: +34 / 93 / 3 19 21 02
www.comerc24.com

Opening hours: Tue–Fri 1.30 pm to 4 pm and 8.30 pm to midnight, Sat 8.30 pm to midnight
Prices: €€
Cuisine: Asian, Andalusian, Catalan, Italian, American
Public transportation: Metro Arc de Triomf   **Map:** No. 3

Eva Padberg's Special Tip

Chef Carles Abellan serves deconstructed tapas, such as poached egg topped with potato-truffle foam and served in its shell.

This gourmet restaurant celebrates food at the highest level without going over the top. Carles Abellan cooks Catalan style but does not shy away from adding Asian, Italian, Andalusian, or even American touches. Where else would you get a hamburger with foie gras pâté and truffles? The atmosphere is what the menu preaches: classic with original accents.

In diesem Gourmet-Restaurant wird Essen auf hohem Niveau zelebriert, ohne dabei die Bodenhaftung zu verlieren. Carles Abellan kocht katalanisch, spielt dabei aber virtuos mit asiatischen, italienischen, andalusischen und sogar amerikanischen Einflüssen. Wo sonst bekommt man schon einen Hamburger mit Foie gras und Trüffeln? Wie die Karte, so das Ambiente: klassisch mit originellen Akzenten.

Ce restaurant gastronomique propose une cuisine de haut niveau à des prix abordables. Carles Abellan cuisine à la catalane mais n'hésite pas à ajouter à ses plats une touche asiatique, italienne, andalouse, voire américaine. Où d'autre pourrait-on trouver un hamburger au foie gras truffé ? L'atmosphère ressemble à la carte : classique avec quelques pointes d'originalité.

En este restaurante de *gourmets* la comida se celebra por todo lo alto sin perderse el contacto con el suelo. Carles Abellan cocina a la catalana jugando virtuosamente con influencias asiáticas, italianas, andaluzas e incluso estadounidenses: ¿dónde, si no, se puede comer una hamburguesa con foie-gras y trufas? A tal carta, tal ambiente: clásico con notas originales.

Cuines Santa Caterina

Avinguada de Francesc
Cambó s/n
08002 Barcelona
Ciutat Vella
Phone: +34 / 93 / 2 68 99 18
www.grupotragaluz.com

Opening hours: Daily 1 pm to 4 pm and 8 pm to 11.30 pm, Tue–Sat to 12.30 am
Prices: €€
Cuisine: Tapas, vegetarian, Oriental, Asian, Mediterranean
Public transportation: Metro Jaume I
Map: No. 4

And now for something completely different, yet truly Spanish: sitting at long tables under fig trees in Cuines Santa Caterina is a convivial kind of experience. If you so wish, you can face the open kitchen. Tapas snacks or à la carte, the choice is yours: sushi or tempura, pasta or paella. Ingredients for seasonal dishes are all fresh, bought directly from the market.

Mal ganz was anderes und doch urspanisch: Im Caterina, das in einer Markthalle liegt, sitzt man an großen Tischen unter Ficusbäumen gesellig zusammen – wer möchte, mit Blick in die offenen Küchen. Im Angebot sind Tapas-Snacks und Essen à la carte: Sushi oder Tempura, Pasta oder Paella. Die Zutaten für die saisonalen Gerichte sind alle frisch und stammen direkt vom Markt.

Avec ses longues tables installées sous les figuiers, Cuines Santa Caterina offre une expérience complètement différente et pourtant authentiquement espagnole, celle de la convivialité. On peut, si on le souhaite, prendre place devant la cuisine ouverte. Tapas ou menu à la carte, on n'a que l'embarras du choix : sushi ou tempura, pâtes ou paella. Les plats de saison sont composés avec des ingrédients frais, achetés directement au marché.

Completamente distinto y, pese a todo, en la tradición del país: en este local, integrado dentro de un mercado, los clientes comparten largas mesas de madera "a la sombra" de ficus o se sientan frente a las cocinas abiertas. La oferta abarca tapas, aperitivos y platos a la carta: *sushi* o *tempura*, pasta o paella. Los ingredientes para las recetas estacionales son todos frescos, directamente del mercado al fogón.

Drolma Restaurant

Hotel Majestic
Passeig de Gràcia, 70
08008 Barcelona
Eixample
Phone: +34 / 93 / 4 96 77 10
www.drolmarestaurant.cat

Opening hours: Mon–Sat 1 pm to 3.30 pm and 8.30 pm to 11 pm, closed on Sun
Prices: €€€€
Cuisine: Catalan, classical cuisine
Public transportation: Metro, bus Passeig de Gràcia
Map: No. 5

Wood-paneled walls, ruby-colored carpet, full-length drapery—you are forgiven for thinking you are in an exclusive London club. Yet the elegant atmosphere only hints at the restaurant's exquisite cuisine, which first opened its doors to the public in 1999. Fermí Puig serves top quality haute cuisine: Catalan culinary tradition refined with French elements. *Chapeau!*

Holzgetäfelte Wände, weinroter Teppich, bodenlange Vorhänge – im ersten Moment glaubt man sich in einen vornehmen britischen Club versetzt. Das elegante Ambiente ist jedoch nur ein kleiner Vorgeschmack auf die exquisite Küche des 1999 eröffneten Restaurants. Fermí Puig tischt Haute Cuisine vom Allerfeinsten auf: katalanische Kochkunst verfeinert mit französischen Elementen. Chapeau!

Boiseries, tapis bordeaux, tentures imposantes, on se croirait dans un club londonien sélect ! L'élégance du décor ne fait que souligner l'excellence de ce restaurant qui a ouvert ses portes au public en 1999. Fermí Puig y sert une cuisine ultra raffinée, mélange de tradition culinaire catalane et d'influences françaises. Chapeau !

Paredes forradas de madera, moqueta de color burdeos, cortinas hasta el suelo: por un momento, uno cree estar en un elegante club británico. El refinado ambiente es sólo un minúsculo anticipo de la exquisita cocina del restaurante, inaugurado en 1999. En él, Fermí Puig ofrece la más depurada haute cuisine: el arte culinario catalán enriquecido con elementos franceses. *Chapeau!*

El Japonés

Passatge Concepció, 2
08008 Barcelona
Eixample
Phone: +34 / 93 / 4 87 25 92
www.eljaponesdeltragaluz.com

Opening hours: Mon–Sun 1.30 pm to 4 pm, Sun–Wed 8.30 pm to midnight and Thu to 12.30 am, Fri–Sat 8 pm to 1 am
Prices: €€
Cuisine: Asian   **Public transportation:** Metro Diagonal   **Map:** No. 6

Russell James' Special Tip
Fashionistas convene at this arty eatery's wooden tables to snack on sushi, noodles and deliciously unusual Japanese pizza. Remember, reservations aren't accepted.

Unadorned long wooden tables, minimalist décor—the interior hints at the concept: functional, puristic, modern, all of which is also reflected in the food. Those who appreciate Asian cuisine but are short on time have hit the jackpot with El Japonés. Here you get fast food of the highest standard: sushi and many other Japanese delicacies at affordable prices.

Schlichte lange Holztische, minimalistische Deko – die Einrichtung verweist auf das Konzept: funktional, puristisch, modern, und das findet seine Entsprechung auch im Essen. Wer die asiatische Küche zu schätzen weiß, aber wenig Zeit hat, der ist im El Japonés genau richtig. Hier gibt es Fastfood auf hohem Niveau: Sushi und viele andere japanische Delikatessen zu vernünftigen Preisen.

Longues tables en bois toutes simples, décoration minimaliste, tout ici se veut fonctionnel, puriste, moderne, concept qui se reflète également dans la carte. Les amateurs de cuisine asiatique qui sont pressés trouveront ici de quoi ravir leurs papilles ; fast food de qualité, avec sushis ou autres mets japonais à des prix raisonnables.

Mesas largas y sobrias de madera, decoración minimalista… El ambiente rubrica el concepto: funcional, purista, moderno, y todo ello con su reflejo en la comida. Para quienes aprecian la cocina asiática, pero tienen poco tiempo, El Japonés es el local ideal, ya que ofrece *fast food* de alta calidad: *sushi* y otras muchas delicias japonesas a precios razonables.

Els Pescadors

Plaça Prim, 1
08005 Barcelona
Sant Martí
Phone: +34 / 93 / 2 25 20 18
www.elspescadors.com

Opening hours: Daily from 1 pm to 3.45 pm and from 8 pm to 11.30 pm
Prices: €€€
Cuisine: Mediterranean, Catalan
Public transportation: Bus Poblenou   **Map:** No. 7

Russell James' Special Tip
Impeccably prepared, just-caught seafood stars at this stylish restaurant outfitted with marble-topped tables and exposed wood beams.

The Els Pescadors in Poble Nou may lie somewhat off the beaten track but it is worth making the effort. It is considered one of Barcelona's best fish restaurants and serves the freshest specialties the sea has to offer in classical Catalan style. The rustic interior—marble counter, tables and rafters are originals and over 100 years old—rounds off the complete feeling of authenticity.

Das Els Pescadors liegt in Poble Nou zwar etwas abseits, ist aber kulinarisch ein Volltreffer. Es gilt als eines der besten Fischrestaurants von Barcelona, hier werden die frischesten Meeresspezialitäten klassisch katalanisch zubereitet. Die rustikale Einrichtung – Marmortheke, Tische und Dachsparren stammen noch aus den Anfängen vor über 100 Jahren – verleiht der Taverne das gewisse authentische Etwas.

Bien que situé un peu à l'écart des sentiers battus, dans le quartier de Poble Nou, Els Pescadors mérite pourtant le détour. Il passe en effet pour l'un des meilleurs restaurants de poisson de Barcelone. D'une fraîcheur irréprochable, les produits de la mer sont ici cuisinés à la catalane. Le décor rustique – comptoir en marbre, tables et poutres ont plus d'un siècle – accentue l'impression de parfaite authenticité.

Aunque un poco fuera de juego por su emplazamiento en Poble Nou, Els Pescadors es una jugada redonda en lo culinario. Está considerado uno de los mejores restaurantes de pescado de Barcelona, donde se preparan las especialidades más frescas a la manera clásica catalana. La decoración rústica –la barra de mármol, las mesas y los cabrios siguen siendo los de los inicios hace más de cien años– confieren al restaurante un cierto carácter de autenticidad.

Flash Flash Tortilleria

Carrer La Granada del Penedès, 25
08006 Barcelona
Gràcia
Phone: +34 / 93 / 2 37 09 90
www.flashflashtortilleria.com

Opening hours: Daily 1 pm to 1.30 am
Prices: €
Cuisine: Omelets, American
Public transportation: Bus Via Augusta – Avinguda Diagonal   **Map:** No. 8

Eva Padberg's Special Tip
Since 1970, this affordable eatery has fed the masses marvelous omelets stuffed with everything from chorizo to brains to cod.

Smile! The model with the camera adorning the walls is Leopoldo Pomés' wife, himself Catalan photographer and cofounder of this funky bar. It is authentic through and through: the pop art ambiance has not been touched since it first opened its doors to the public in 1970. The specialty of the house are hamburgers and more than 70 different kinds of omelets—some of them pretty elaborate.

Bitte lächeln! Das Model mit der Kamera, das die Wände schmückt, war die Frau von Leopoldo Pomés, katalanischer Fotograf und Mitbegründer des funkigen Lokals. Es ist authentisch durch und durch, denn seit der Eröffnung 1970 ist nichts am Pop-Art-Ambiente verändert worden. Spezialität des Hauses sind Hamburger und mehr als 70 verschiedene zum Teil sehr raffinierte Omelettsorten.

Souriez ! Le mannequin, qui brandit l'appareil photo et orne le mur, était l'épouse de Leopoldo Pomés, lui-même photographe catalan et cofondateur de ce bar branché. Tout est resté authentique, l'ambiance pop art est demeurée intacte depuis son ouverture en 1970. Parmi les spécialités maison, les hamburgers et plus de 70 sortes d'omelettes, dont certaines très sophistiquées.

¡Una sonrisita! La modelo con la cámara que decora las paredes estuvo casada con Leopoldo Pomés, fotógrafo catalán y cofundador de este local de moda. Su ambiente Pop Art es cien por cien auténtico, pues no se ha modificado lo más mínimo desde su fundación en 1970. La especialidad de la casa son las hamburguesas y más de setenta modalidades distintas de tortilla, algunas realmente sofisticadas.

Il Giardinetto

Carrer La Granada del Penedès, 22
08006 Barcelona
Eixample
Phone: +34 / 93 / 2 18 75 36
www.ilgiardinetto.es

Opening hours: Daily from 1.30 pm to 4.30 pm and from 8.30 pm to 1.30 am
Prices: €€
Cuisine: Italian
Public transportation: Bus Via Augusta – Avinguda Diagonal
Map: No. 9

If you step through the doors of Il Giardinetto you are forgiven for thinking you walked straight into somebody's garden. Different hues of green on the walls and ceiling dictate the interior. The restaurant has not lost any of its charm since it opened in 1974. Apart from excellent Italian pasta dishes you can also enjoy an evening with a cocktail, listening to piano music.

Wer durch die Tür des Il Giardinetto tritt, der hat den Eindruck, direkt in einem Garten gelandet zu sein. Verschiedene Grüntöne an Wänden und Decke bestimmen das Bild. Das Restaurant, das bereits 1974 eröffnet wurde, hat seitdem nichts von seinem Charme verloren. Neben den hervorragenden italienischen Pastakreationen kann man am Abend auch entspannt einen Cocktail zur Pianomusik genießen.

En franchissant les portes d'Il Giardinetto, on a l'impression de pénétrer dans un véritable jardin. Et c'est bien normal dans ce décor où, des murs au plafond, le vert domine dans toutes ses déclinaisons. Le restaurant n'a rien perdu de son charme depuis son ouverture en 1974. On peut y déguster de délicieuses pâtes italiennes ou bien alors passer la soirée à siroter un cocktail en écoutant du piano.

Quien traspasa el umbral de Il Giardinetto tiene la impresión de haber ido a parar a un jardín. Los distintos tonos de verde en las paredes y techos dan al lugar su característica imagen. Este restaurante inaugurado en 1974 no ha perdido desde entonces nada de su encanto. Además de sus excelentes creaciones de pasta italianas, por la noche ofrece la posibilidad de disfrutar de un coctel en un ambiente íntimo amenizado por música de piano.

Marmalade

Riera Alta, 4-6
08001 Barcelona
Raval
Phone: +34 / 93 / 4 42 39 66
www.marmaladebarcelona.com

Opening hours: Mon–Sun from 7 am to 3 am, daily Happy Hour from 7 pm to 9 pm, Brunch Sun 11 am to 4 pm
Prices: €€
Cuisine: Gourmet style Tapas and Mediterranean
Public transportation: Metro Liceu, Sant Antoni
Map: No. 10

Like its older sister, the Milk, the 300 meters squared (3230-square-feet) Marmalade is not shy when it comes to showing off. Thick oriental carpets, heavy sofas, and copper-plated walls effuse nostalgic nonchalance. The huge hand-carved billiard table and the 13-feet long chromed art deco bar are reminiscent of 1950s Havana.

Das Marmalade geizt wie seine ältere Schwester, das Milk, nicht mit seinen Reizen. Dicke Orientteppiche, schwere Sofas und mit Kupfer verkleidete Wände verbreiten nostalgische Lässigkeit. Der handgeschnitzte riesige Billardtisch und die vier Meter lange verchromte Bar im Art-déco-Stil geben dem 300 Quadratmeter großen Restaurant einen Hauch von Havanna in den Fünfzigern.

Tout comme son grand frère le Milk, le Marmalade, avec ses 300 mètres carrés, ne craint pas d'étaler son luxe. Epais tapis orientaux, canapés profonds, murs revêtus de cuivre – tout ici respire une nostalgique nonchalance. L'immense table de billard sculptée à la main et le bar chromé art déco de 4 mètres de long évoquent La Havane des années cinquante.

Marmalade, al igual que su hermana mayor, Milk, no escatima en encanto: voluminosas alfombras orientales, grandes sofás y recubrimientos de cobre en las paredes contagian un desenfado nostálgico. La enorme mesa de billar tallada a mano y la barra de cuatro metros de estilo Art Déco contribuyen a que en este restaurante de 300 metros cuadrados se respire un cierto aire de La Habana de los cincuenta.

Negro

Avinguda Diagonal, 640
08017 Barcelona
Les Corts
Phone: +34 / 93 / 4 05 94 94
www.negrodeltragaluz.com

Opening hours: Mon–Fri 1.30 pm to 4 pm, Sun–Wed 8.30 pm to midnight, Thu–Sat 8.30 pm to 1 am
Prices: €
Cuisine: Japanese Tapas
Public transportation: Bus Avinguda Diagonal-Entença
Map: No. 11

This is where hip city slickers hang out for lunch, dinner or just a drink. The Negro, located on one of the city's two main boulevards, the Avinguda Diagonal, is one of the hippest and most modern bars and restaurants. Snazzy light furniture, unobtrusive decorations and a few light effects—not too little to be boring, not too busy to be obtrusive. Understatement à la Barcelona.

Hierher kommen hippe Großstädter zum Mittagessen, Abendessen oder auf einen Drink. Das an einem der beiden großen Boulevards der Stadt, der Avinguda Diagonal, gelegene Negro gehört zu den sehr modernen Bars und Restaurants. Schicke leichte Möbel, dezente Deko, ein paar Lichteffekte – nicht zuwenig, um langweilig, nicht zuviel, um aufdringlich zu wirken. Understatement à la Barcelona.

C'est le lieu d'élection des Barcelonais branchés, qui viennent ici déjeuner, dîner ou simplement prendre un verre. Situé sur l'Avinguda Diagonal, l'une des deux grandes artères de la ville, le Negro est l'un des bars-restaurants actuellement les plus en vue. Mobilier chic et léger, décoration discrète, quelques effets de lumière, ni trop ni trop peu pour ne pas lasser ni importuner le client. Un pur euphémisme à la Barcelonaise.

A este local acude la gente guapa de la ciudad a comer, cenar o tomar unas copas. Negro, que está en la Diagonal, una de las dos grandes avenidas de la ciudad, se cuenta entre los bares y restaurantes más de vanguardia. Elegantes muebles ligeros, decoración discreta, algunos efectos lumínicos: lo justo para que no resulte aburrido ni llegue a ser abrumador. Sobriedad a la barcelonesa.

Torre d'Alta Mar

Passeig de Joan de Borbó, 88
08023 Barcelona
Ciutat Vella
Phone: +34 / 93 / 2 21 00 07
www.torredealtamar.com

Opening hours: Mon 7 pm to 11.30 pm, Tue–Sat 1 pm to 3.30 pm and 7 pm to 11.30 pm
Prices: €€€€
Cuisine: Catalan, Mediterranean
Public transportation: Metro Barceloneta
Map: No. 12

The Torre d'Alta Mar is not only a culinary highlight: its unique location in a 246-feet tall cable car tower Torre Sant Sebastià proffers breathtaking panoramic views over the city and its port. The innovative cuisine combines Catalan classics, especially fish, with other Mediterranean influences.

Das Torre d'Alta Mar ist nicht nur in kulinarischer Hinsicht ein Hochgenuss: Die einzigartige Lage im 75 Meter hohen Seilbahnturm Torre Sant Sebastià bietet einen atemberaubenden Panoramablick über Stadt und Hafen. Die innovative Küche kombiniert katalanische Klassiker, vor allem Fisch, mit Einflüssen anderer mediterraner Länder.

La Torre d'Alta Mar n'est pas seulement un haut lieu de la gastronomie, c'est un endroit unique situé au sommet d'un pylône de téléphérique de 75 mètres de haut. La Torre Sant Sebastià offre une vue panoramique à couper le souffle sur la ville et le port. Innovante, la cuisine combine les ingrédients traditionnels de la cuisine catalane, notamment le poisson, avec d'autres influences méditerranéennes.

Torre d'Alta Mar no sólo es una delicia en el aspecto culinario. Desde su espléndido emplazamiento a 75 metros de altura en la Torre Sant Sebastià del transbordador aéreo del puerto se obtiene una panorámica impresionante de la ciudad y el puerto. Su innovadora cocina armoniza los clásicos catalanes, sobre todo de pescado, con elementos de otros países mediterráneos.

Tragaluz

Passatge de la Concepció, 5
08008 Barcelona
Eixample
Phone: +34 / 93 / 4 87 06 21
www.grupotragaluz.com

Opening hours: Daily 1.30 pm to 4 pm, Sun–Wed 8.30 pm to midnight, Thu–Sat 8.30 pm to 1 am
Prices: €€€€
Cuisine: Mediterranean, avant-garde cuisine
Public transportation: Metro Diagonal
Map: No. 13

The flagship of the Grupo Tragaluz oozes a special charm thanks to its creative cuisine and its outstanding location. The movable glass saddle roof creates light effects on all three levels. An eye catcher is an oak tree trunk with an aluminum spiral staircase winding itself around it. On the ground floor, guests witness the making of sushi and tempura in front of their eyes. The restaurant is on the second level.

Seinen Charme verdankt das Flaggschiff der Grupo Tragaluz der kreativen Küche und der besonderen Location. Das bewegliche Giebeldach aus Glas sorgt für Lichteffekte auf allen drei Ebenen. Blickfang ist ein Eichenstamm, um den sich eine Aluminium-Wendeltreppe windet. Im Untergeschoss wird vor den Augen der Gäste Sushi und Tempura zubereitet, auf der zweiten Ebene befindet sich das Restaurant.

Une cuisine créative, un emplacement exceptionnel, voilà ce qui fait le charme du vaisseau amiral du Grupo Tragaluz. Un toit en verre coulissant crée des effets de lumière sur les trois niveaux, et un étonnant escalier en colimaçon s'enroule autour d'un chêne. Au rez-de-chaussée, sushis et tempuras sont confectionnés sous les yeux des convives. Le restaurant se trouve au second niveau.

El atractivo del buque insignia del Grupo Tragaluz descansa en su cocina y su privilegiada localización. El techo movible acristalado crea efectos lumínicos en las tres plantas del local. Uno de sus centros de atención es un tronco de roble alrededor del cual asciende una escalera de caracol de aluminio. En la planta baja se prepara sushi y tempura a la vista de los comensales. En la planta superior se encuentra el restaurante.

CLUBS, LOUNGES & BARS

Angels & Kings

ME Barcelona
Avinguda Diagonal, 272-286 / Pere IV
08005 Barcelona
Sant Martí
Phone: +34 / 93 / 3 67 20 50
www.mebymelia.com
www.angelsandkings.com

Opening hours: Thu–Sat 10 pm to 5 am, Tue and Wed 10 pm to 3 am
Prices: €€€€
Public transportation: Metro Poblenou
Map: No. 14

It started with alternative rock musician Pete Wentz, bass player of the band Fall Out Boy, looking for a cool place for him and his gang to hang out. The rest is history: he opened the first night club in New York, followed by places in Chicago and Barcelona. Black walls, glass chandeliers and vintage furniture create a modern yet relaxed hot spot in the five-star hotel ME.

Eigentlich suchte Alternativrocker Pete Wentz, Bassist der Band Fall Out Boy, nur einen Platz zum Abhängen für sich und seine Jungs. Der Rest ist Geschichte: In New York eröffnete er den ersten Nachtclub, es folgten Chicago und Barcelona. Schwarze Wände, Glaslüster und Vintagemöbel machen die Location im 5-Sterne-Hotel ME zu einem modernen, aber entspannten Hotspot.

Tout a commencé à l'époque où Pete Wentz, le musicien de rock alternatif – bassiste du groupe Fall Out Boy – cherchait un local où se produire avec ses acolytes. La suite fait partie de l'histoire : il ouvrit la première boîte de nuit à New York et les suivantes à Chicago et Barcelone. Murs noirs, lustres en verre, mobilier vintage, un lieu à la fois moderne et décontracté dans l'enceinte de l'hôtel cinq étoiles ME.

En realidad, Pete Wentz, roquero alternativo bajista de Fall Out Boy, sólo buscaba un lugar donde poder desconectar con su grupo. El resto es historia: abrió el primer club nocturno en Nueva York, al que siguieron el de Chicago y el de Barcelona. Paredes negras, arañas de cristal y muebles vintage convierten este local ubicado en el Hotel ME, de cinco estrellas, en un club moderno, pero relajante.

Boadas Cocktail Bar

Carrer dels Tallers, 1
08001 Barcelona
Ciutat Vella
Phone: +34 / 93 / 3 18 88 26

Opening hours: Mon–Thu noon to 2 am, Fri+Sat noon to 3 am, legal holidays noon to 3 pm
and 6 pm to 2 am, closed on Sun
Prices: €€
Public transportation: Metro Catalunya
Map: No. 15

Here's looking at you, kid: Humphrey Bogart would have felt at home in Boadas. Opened in 1933, the
small and intimate place is supposedly Barcelona's oldest cocktail bar. The owner learned his trade in
Ernest Hemingway's legendary local El Floridita in Havana. To this day the drinks with English gin, Carib-
bean rum and Russian vodka are among the best Barcelona has to offer.

Ich schau' dir in die Augen, Kleines: Ins Boadas hätte auch Humphrey Bogart gepasst. 1933 eröffnet,
gilt die kleine, intime Location als älteste Cocktailbar der Stadt. Sein Handwerk lernte der Begründer
in Ernest Hemingways legendärer Stammkneipe El Floridita in Havanna. Und noch heute gehören die
Drinks mit englischem Gin, karibischem Rum und russischem Wodka zu den Besten der Stadt.

« 'T'as d'beaux yeux, tu sais' ». L'Humphrey Bogart de Casablanca se serait senti chez lui au Boadas.
Fondé en 1933, ce petit local intime passe pour l'un des plus anciens bars à cocktails de Barcelone.
Le propriétaire a appris le métier au Floridita, bar légendaire d'Hemingway à La Havane. Aujourd'hui
encore, les cocktails à base de gin anglais, de rhum des Caraïbes et de vodka russe sont parmi les
meilleurs de la ville.

"Mírame a los ojos, pequeña": Boadas habría hecho las delicias de Humphrey Bogart. Inaugurado en
1933, este pequeño e íntimo establecimiento es uno de los bares de cócteles más antiguos de la
ciudad. Su fundador aprendió su oficio en La Habana, en El Floridita, el legendario local del que era
asiduo Ernest Hemingway. Y sus combinados de ginebra inglesa, ron caribeño y vodka ruso se cuentan
todavía hoy entre los mejores de la ciudad.

CDLC

Passeig Marìtim, 32
08005 Barcelona
Ciutat Vella
Phone: +34 / 93 / 2 24 04 70
www.cdlcbarcelona.com

Opening hours: Daily 2 pm to 3 am
Prices: €€€
Public transportation: Metro Ciutadella Vila Olímpica
Map: No. 16

Prices and snob factor hit the roof. But that is part and parcel of enjoying Barcelona's hottest club. To see and be seen is the be all and end all in the CDLC—here you will come face to face with plenty of soccer VIPs. In the afternoon you can relax in leather sofas as big as beds under two massive bedouin tents. At night the club turns into a funky party zone. Dress code!

Die Preise sind hoch, der Snob-Faktor auch. Aber das gehört sich nun mal für einen der heißesten Clubs der Stadt. Sehen und gesehen werden ist im CDLC die Devise, viele Fußball-VIPs geben sich hier die Klinke in die Hand. Nachmittags relaxt man unter zwei riesigen Beduinenzelten auf Ledersofas so groß wie Betten, nachts wird der Club zur funkigen Partyzone. Dresscode!

C'est le lieu le plus cher et le plus snob de Barcelone, mais c'est justement pour cela qu'on l'aime. Voir et être vu, c'est avant tout ce que l'on recherche au CDLC, où l'on croise fréquemment de nombreuses personnalités du football. L'après-midi, on peut se détendre sous d'immenses tentes de bédouins, dans des canapés en cuir extra larges. Le soir en revanche, le club est réservé aux inconditionnels de la danse. Tenue correcte exigée !

Los precios son elevados, tanto como su esnobismo. Pero no podría ser de otro modo en uno de los locales más en boga de la ciudad. En CDLC, la consigna es ver y dejarse ver. Muchos VIPs del mundo futbolístico integran la lista de sus habituales. Por la tarde, uno puede relajarse bajo dos enormes carpas beduinas en sofás de piel tan grandes como camas; por la noche, el club se convierte en un lugar de marcha con mucho ritmo. ¡Se pide corrección en el vestir!

Elephant

Passeig dels Tilers, 1
08034 Barcelona
Les Corts
Phone: +34 / 93 / 3 34 02 58
www.elephantbcn.com

Opening hours: Thu, Fri and Sat 11.30 pm to 5.30 am
Prices: €€€
Public transportation: Metro Palau Reial
Map: No. 17

Chic, exclusive and not exactly cheap, but the outlandish atmosphere is worth every cent. Once inside you are forgiven for thinking you've just entered Scheherazade's Arabian Nights. Colonial style furniture, golden elephants, an exotic garden, and many other Far Eastern influences help to create the perfect oriental illusion. All that is missing is a genie...

Chic, exklusiv und nicht ganz billig, aber das ausgefallene Ambiente ist jeden Cent wert. Kaum eingetreten, fühlt man sich wie in einem Märchen aus Tausendundeiner Nacht. Möbel im Kolonialstil, goldene Elefanten, ein exotisch dekorierter Garten und viele andere fernöstliche Stilelemente schaffen die perfekte orientalische Illusion. Fehlt nur noch, dass plötzlich ein Flaschengeist auftaucht…

Chic, sélect et pas exactement abordable, mais le décor vaut vraiment le coup d'œil. Car il suffit de mettre le pied à l'Eléphant pour avoir l'impression de pénétrer dans un conte des Mille et une nuits. Mobilier colonial, éléphants dorés, jardin au décor exotique et bien d'autres influences encore contribuent à créer la parfaite illusion orientale. Ne manque que le génie de la lampe…

Elegante, exclusivo y no precisamente barato, aunque su insólito ambiente bien lo merece. Nada más entrar, uno se siente como en un cuento de Las mil y una noches. Muebles de estilo colonial, elefantes dorados, un jardín exóticamente decorado y otros muchos elementos estilísticos del Lejano Oriente logran recrear una perfecta ilusión oriental. Sólo falta el genio saliendo de la lámpara maravillosa…

G-Bar

Carrer d'Enric Granados, 83
08008 Barcelona
Eixample
Phone: +34 / 93 / 4 92 96 70
www.derbyhotels.com

Opening hours: Daily from 11 am to noon, G-Bar Terrace Mon–Thu 6 pm to 1 am and Fri–Sun 6 pm to 1.30 am
Prices: €€€€
Public transportation: Metro Diagonal and Passeig de Gràcia
Map: No. 18

The boutique hotel Granados 83 has more to offer than just luxurious and stylish accommodation. The hotel's own G-Bar shakes and stirs cocktails throughout the year. The modern minimalist bar is home to an international audience, but locals also take advantage of the wonderful drinks and trendy atmosphere.

Das Boutique-Hotel Granados 83 bietet nicht nur luxuriöse und stylische Übernachtungsmöglichkeiten. In der Hotelbar G-Bar werden das ganze Jahr über Cocktails gerührt und geschüttelt. In der modern minimalistisch eingerichteten Bar trifft sich ein internationales Publikum, aber auch Einheimische wissen die gut gemixten Drinks und die trendige Atmosphäre zu schätzen.

Le « boutique hôtel » Granados 83 a beaucoup plus à offrir qu'un hébergement de luxe. Son G-Bar concocte une sélection de cocktails tout au long de l'année. On trouvera dans ce décor moderne et minimaliste une clientèle internationale, mais aussi les Barcelonais qui apprécient les cocktails préparés avec art et l'atmosphère « tendance » du lieu.

El selecto Hotel Granados 83 no sólo brinda la posibilidad de pernoctar en un lujoso ambiente de diseño. En G-Bar, el bar del hotel, se mezclan y agitan cócteles durante todo el año. En este local de moderna decoración minimalista se reúne un público internacional, aunque también los barceloneses saben valorar sus excelentes combinados y su atmósfera vanguardista.

Lotus Theater

Calle Bailén, 22
08010 Barcelona
Eixample
Phone: +34 / 90 / 2 62 79 87
www.lotustheater.info

Opening hours: Mon–Sun midnight to 5 am
Prices: €€
Public transportation: Metro Arc de Triomf (exit Av. de Vilanova), Plaza Tetuán, Urquinaona
Map: No. 19

Russell James' Special Tip
If you're ready to dance till dawn, this sultry club mixes go-go girls with raucous bands, cabaret acts and first-rate DJs.

Once home to Spain's best-known peepshow, now a place of culture. "Welcome, bienvenue, Willkommen…!" is the motto the Lotus Theater follows almost every night. Small premieres, stand up comedy or cabaret—you will find it here. But the focus lies on live music: the Lotus offers its stage to famous soloists and bands but also to up-and-comers.

Wo früher Spaniens bekannteste Peepshow lockte, wird jetzt Kultur geboten. „Willkommen, bienvenue, welcome…!" heißt es fast jeden Abend im Lotus Theater. Es gibt kleine Theateraufführungen, Stand-Up Comedy und Cabaret-Shows zu sehen. Der Schwerpunkt liegt aber auf Livemusik: Das Lotus bietet bekannten Solisten und Gruppen, aber auch Newcomern eine Plattform.

Peepshow jadis le plus célèbre d'Espagne, c'est aujourd'hui un lieu de culture. « Welcome, bienvenue, Willkommen…! », tel est le mot d'ordre du Lotus Theater presque tous les soirs. Spectacles courts, stand up, cabaret… tous les genres sont ici représentés. Mais priorité est donnée aux concerts live : le Lotus accueille sur sa scène des chanteurs et groupes célèbres, mais aussi des nouveaux venus.

Donde en el pasado fue protagonista el erotismo, hoy se ofrece cultura. "Willkommen, bienvenue, welcome…", así empieza el espectáculo casi todas las noches en el Lotus Theater, donde se pueden ver pequeñas representaciones teatrales, arte cómico y espectáculos de cabaret. Con todo, su punto fuerte es la música en directo: el Lotus ofrece una plataforma a los mejores solistas y grupos, pero también a nuevas promesas.

Milk

Carrer d'En Gignàs, 21
08002 Barcelona
Barri Gòtic
Phone: +34 / 93 / 2 68 09 22
www.milkbarcelona.com

Opening hours: Mon–Fri 6 pm to 3 am, Sat and Sun 11 am to 3 am, daily Happy Hour 7 pm to 9 pm, Brunch Sat+Sun 11 am to 4 pm
Prices: €€
Public transportation: Metro Jaume I   **Map:** No. 20

Russell James' Special Tip
From 7pm to 9pm daily, this chic cocktail lounge's potent libations, like the citrusy Whiskey Savage, cost €3.50.

Opened in 2005, the Milk in the El Gòtic neighborhood counts among the city's hippest cocktail bars. Is it simply nostalgia or is it the fact that it is like going back in time to the good old days? Comfy sofas, gilded picture frames, and antique chandeliers exude luxurious comfort. The wallpaper with a floral pattern and egrets in typical '50s style by designer Florence Broadhurst rounds up the cool Bohemian style.

2005 eröffnet, ist das Milk im Viertel El Gòtic heute eine der angesagtesten Cocktailbars der Stadt. Ob's am Nostalgiefaktor liegt? Man fühlt sich hier jedenfalls wie in die gute alte Zeit zurückversetzt. Gemütliche Sofas, vergoldete Bilderrahmen und ein antiker Lüster verströmen luxuriöse Behaglichkeit. Die Tapete mit Blumenmuster und Reihern der Designerin Florence Broadhurst im Stil der 50er-Jahre rundet den lässigen Bohème-Stil ab.

Ouvert en 2005 et situé dans le quartier El Gòtic, le Milk est l'un des bars à cocktails les plus branchés de la ville. Est-ce l'effet de la nostalgie ou alors sommes-nous revenus au bon vieux temps ? Divans moelleux, cadres dorés à l'or fin, lustre ancien – tout ici respire le confort luxueux. Imaginé par la décoratrice Florence Broadhurst, le papier peint, avec ses motifs de fleurs et d'aigrettes typiques des années cinquante, renforce l'impression bohème et décontractée du lieu.

Inaugurado en 2005 en el Barri Gòtic, Milk es uno de los bares de cócteles más de moda de la ciudad. Quizás esto se deba al factor nostalgia, ya que en este local uno se siente como transportado a los buenos viejos tiempos. Sofás confortables, marcos dorados y una antigua araña crean un ambiente de serenidad lujosa. Empapelados con motivos florales y garzas en estilo de los años cincuenta de la diseñadora Florence Broadhurst redondean su desenfadado estilo bohemio.

Otto Zutz

Carrer de Lincoln, 15
08006 Barcelona
Gràcia
Phone: +34 / 93 / 2 38 07 22
www.ottozutz.es

Opening hours: Tue–Wed midnight to 5 am and Thu–Sat midnight to 5.30 am
Prices: €€€
Public transportation: Bus Via Augusta – Princep d'Astúries
Map: No. 21

Eva Padberg's Special Tip
Sweet-talk your way into one of this pulsing, packed nightclub's VIP cards and, from the exclusive third floor, you can overlook the shimmying dancers.

It's party time! Fans of house, hip-hop, or R'n'B, who like to dance the whole night through, simply must check out this club—one of Barcelona's oldest. Each of the three levels plays different music to dance and pose to until you drop. Every Thursday the owners organize parties with the cream of the crop of national and international DJs behind the turntables.

It's Partytime! Wer auf House, Hip Hop oder R'n'B steht und gern die Nächte durchtanzt, kommt am Zutz, einem der ältesten Clubs der Stadt, nicht vorbei. Auf jeder der drei Etagen wird zu anderer Musik rund um die Uhr getanzt und gepost, was das Zeug hält. Donnerstags organisieren die Betreiber Partys mit den besten nationalen und internationalen DJs an den Turntables.

C'est la fête ! Pour les amateurs de house, hip hop ou R'n'B, qui aiment danser jusqu'au bout de la nuit, ce club est tout simplement incontournable. A chaque étage son style de musique, avec partout le même mot d'ordre : la danse ! Tous les jeudis, les propriétaires organisent des soirées, conviant aux platines les meilleurs DJ nationaux et internationaux.

It's partytime! Los aficionados al house, el hip-hop o el R&B que disfrutan bailando toda la noche no pasan de largo por el Zutz, uno de los clubes más antiguos de la ciudad. En sus tres plantas con música distinta se baila y se posa mientras el cuerpo aguanta. Los jueves sus gestores organizan fiestas con los mejores DJs nacionales a cargo de los platos giradiscos.

SHOPS

Au nom de la rose

Carrer de València, 203
08007 Barcelona
Eixample
Phone: +34 / 93 / 4 51 16 50
www.aunomdelarose.com

Opening hours: Mon–Fri 9 am to 8.45 pm, Sat 9 am to 2.30 pm and 5 pm to 8.45 pm, Sun 10 am to 2.30 pm
Products: Flowers, decoration, soaps, delicacies
Public transportation: Bus València – Balmes   **Map:** No. 22

Eva Padberg's Special Tip
Follow the colorful petals strewn on the sidewalk into this florist specializing in roses of every conceivable hue.

The name says it all: this exclusive boutique renders homage to the queen of flowers. Apart from roses of all colors it boasts fragrant soaps and candles, tasty jams, chocolates, and syrups. There is a good reason for its French flair: the idea originated in Paris, where the first shop was opened in 1991. Already two branches have opened in Barcelona. *Très chic!*

Der Name ist Programm: Die edle Boutique huldigt der Königin der Blumen in jeder Form. Neben Rosen in allen Farben gibt es duftende Seifen und Kerzen, leckere Marmeladen, Schokoladen und Sirup. Das französische Flair kommt nicht von ungefähr: Die Idee stammt aus Paris, wo 1991 das erste Geschäft gegründet wurde. Barcelona hat inzwischen zwei Rosen-Shops. Très chic!

Comme son nom l'indique, cette élégante boutique rend hommage à la reine des fleurs. Outre des roses de toutes les couleurs, on y trouve des savons et des bougies parfumés, mais aussi une sélection de délicieux produits : confitures, chocolats, sirops. Si l'atmosphère est indéniablement française, c'est que le concept a vu le jour à Paris, où la première boutique a ouvert ses portes en 1991. Deux autres sont aujourd'hui installées à Barcelone. Très chic !

El nombre es todo un programa: esta noble boutique homenajea a la reina de las flores de todas las maneras imaginables. Además de rosas de todos los colores, hay jabones y velas perfumadas, sabrosas mermeladas, chocolates y jarabes. Su ambiente francés no es fortuito: la idea procede de París, donde en 1991 se inauguró la primera tienda. Barcelona tiene actualmente dos boutiques de rosas. *Très chic!*

au nom de la

Vos bouquets livrés partout en France en 24

4,5€

au nom de la rose

Blow by Le Swing

Carrer del Doctor Dou, 11
08001 Barcelona
Ciutat Vella
Phone: +34 / 93 / 3 02 36 98
www.leswingvintage.com

Opening hours: Mon–Sat 10.30 am to 2.30 pm and 4.30 pm to 8.30 pm
Products: Fashion, accessories, furniture
Public transportation: Metro Catalunya, Liceu
Map: No. 23

Those looking for something special will feel at home in Le Swing. The sharp boutique offers everything for the glamour girl—extravagant apparel and shoes from top labels such as Chanel, Dior, or Versace, extravagant hats, purses, and earrings but also kitschy yet nice home accessories. And there is also retro-chic by local designers. Less is more? Forget it: style up your life!

Wer etwas Besonderes sucht, muss sich im Le Swing nicht besonders anstrengen. Die schrille Boutique bietet alles, was das Glamourherz begehrt – extravagante Kleider und Schuhe von Luxuslabels wie Chanel, Dior oder Versace, ausgefallene Hüte, Taschen und Ohrringe, aber auch kitschig-schöne Wohnaccessoires. Außerdem gibt's Retro-Chic lokaler Designer. Weniger ist mehr? Von wegen: Style up your Life!

Qui cherche quelque chose de spécial trouvera ici son bonheur. Chaussures et vêtements extravagants griffés Chanel, Dior, Versace, accessoires originaux – chapeaux, sacs à main, boucles d'oreilles – c'est ici tout l'arsenal glamour qui s'offre à vous, mais aussi une jolie sélection d'articles kitsch pour la maison, sans oublier un choix de tenues chic et rétro dessinées par des stylistes locaux. Soignez votre style !

Los que buscan algo especial no necesitan marearse mucho en Le Swing. Esta insólita boutique ofrece todo lo que anhela un alma glamorosa: extravagantes vestidos y zapatos de marcas lujosas como Chanel, Dior o Versace; llamativos sombreros, bolsos y pendientes, e incluso accesorios de decoración de un kitsch seductor. Además, hay artículos retro-chic de diseñadores locales. ¿Menos es más? Qué va: ¡dale estilo a tu vida!

Blow

by Le Swing

Caelum

Carrer de la Palla, 8
08002 Barcelona
Barri Gòtic
Phone: +34 / 93 / 3 02 69 93

Opening hours: Mon 5 pm to 10:30 pm, Tue–Thu 10.30 am to 8.30 pm, Fri + Sat 10.30 am to midnight
Products: Jams, preserved fruit, quality cakes, biscuits, marzipan and liqueurs
Public transportation: Metro Liceu
Map: No. 24

For those with a sweet tooth, heaven on earth is only a stone's throw away from the Gothic cathedral: in Caelum you will find delicious cakes, marzipan, honey, exclusive wines, liqueurs, and olive oils—all prepared following ancient recipes by nuns and monks. Try the fantastically renovated medieval crypt and relax over a coffee by candlelight.

Nur einen Steinwurf von der gotischen Kathedrale entfernt, tut sich für Genießer der Himmel auf Erden auf: Caelum bietet leckere Kuchen, Marzipan und Honig, edle Weine, Liköre und Olivenöle – alles nach alten Rezepturen von Nonnen und Mönchen hergestellt. In der einzigartig restaurierten mittelalterlichen Krypta kann man bei Kaffee und Kerzenschein entspannen.

À deux pas de la cathédrale gothique, Caelum est un paradis pour les gourmands avec une sélection de gâteaux plus délicieux les uns que les autres, de massepains, de miels, de vins, de liqueurs et d'huiles d'olive, tous fabriqués à partir d'anciennes recettes élaborées par des nonnes et des moines. Dans cette crypte superbement rénovée, vous dégusterez votre café à la lumière des chandelles.

No lejos de la catedral gótica, las puertas del cielo se abren para todos los sibaritas terrenales: Caelum ofrece deliciosos pasteles, mazapanes, miel, vinos nobles, licores y aceite de oliva, todo ello elaborado según antiguas recetas de monjas y monjes. En la cripta medieval, espléndidamente restaurada, se puede hacer un alto en el camino tomando café a la luz de las velas.

Casa Munich

Avinguda Diagonal, 557
08029 Barcelona
Les Corts
Phone: +34 / 93 / 4 10 04
www.munichsports.com

Opening hours: Mon–Sat 10 am to 9.30 pm
Products: Sports and fashion shoes
Public transportation: Bus Access l'Illa
Map: No. 25

Eva Padberg's Special Tip
Snag cool, colorful, limited-edition releases of Munich's legendary Catalan sneakers at this brand-new shop.

This shop is an essential stopover for all sneaker fans. Not only in Spain Casa Munich has attained cult status. The family-run company, founded in Barcelona in 1939, positioned itself on the international market with their characteristic X-logo during the '70s. Today, the venerable Catalan brand is a trendy label throughout the world.

Dieser Shop ist ein unentbehrlicher Zwischenstopp für alle Sneaker-Fans. Nicht nur in Spanien hat Casa Munich Kultstatus erreicht. Die 1939 in Barcelona entstandene Firma, die immer noch in Familienbesitz ist, hat sich in den 70er Jahren mit ihrem charakteristischen X-Logo international positioniert. Heute ist die katalanische Traditionsmarke ein weltweites Trendlabel.

Fans de baskets et autres chaussures de sport, ce magasin est fait pour vous. Mais Casa Munich rayonne aujourd'hui bien au-delà de l'Espagne. Fondée à Barcelone en 1939, cette entreprise familiale s'est positionnée sur le marché international dans les années soixante-dix, en créant son célèbre logo en forme de X. Aujourd'hui, la vénérable marque catalane est devenue tendance dans le monde entier.

Este comercio es una dirección obligada para todos los amantes de las zapatillas de deporte. Casa Munich ha alcanzado estatus de culto no sólo en España. La empresa, nacida en Barcelona en 1939 y de propiedad familiar, se posicionó internacionalmente en la década de 1970 con su logo X. En la actualidad, esta marca tradicional catalana imprime la pauta en la moda a nivel internacional.

hoss intropia

Passeig de Gràcia, 44
08007 Barcelona
Eixample
Phone: + 34 / 93 / 2 72 65 94
www.hossintropia.com

Opening hours: Mon–Sat 10.30 am to 9 pm
Products: Fashion
Public transportation: Metro Passeig de Gràcia
Map: No. 26

A Spanish brand with a cosmopolitan philosophy: the label, established in Madrid in 1994, boasts original women's fashions. Despite the abundance of detail, they are very wearable. The company's social endeavor to aid homeless women is reflected in their pricing: their products are affordable. Apart from its flagship store, Barcelona has one other shop and an outlet.

Spanisch die Marke, kosmopolitisch die Philosophie: Das 1994 in Madrid gegründete Label kleidet Frauen originell und detailverliebt, aber trotzdem tragbar ein. Die soziale Einstellung des Unternehmens – es unterstützt obdachlose Frauen – spiegelt sich auch in der Preispolitik wider: Die Stücke sind durchaus bezahlbar. Neben dem Flagshipstore gibt es in Barcelona noch einen Shop und ein Outlet.

Marque espagnole à la philosophie cosmopolite, hoss intropia, fondée à Madrid en 1994, propose aux femmes une mode originale, facile à porter malgré l'abondance de détails. Le positionnement social de l'entreprise, qui apporte son soutien aux femmes sans domicile fixe, se reflète dans la politique des prix : les articles sont très abordables. La marque dispose actuellement à Barcelone d'un grand magasin, d'une boutique et d'un point de vente.

Empresa española, filosofía cosmopolita: esta marca de ropa creada en Madrid en 1994 viste a la mujer con prendas originales que cuidan los detalles, pero llevables. El compromiso social de la empresa –que apoya a mujeres sin techo– se refleja también en la política de precios: las prendas son completamente asequibles. Además del local insignia, en Barcelona hay otra tienda y un punto de venta.

Iguapop Shop

Carrer del Comerç, 15
08003 Barcelona
Ciutat Vella
Phone Gallery: +34 / 933 10 07 35
Phone Shop: +34 / 93 / 3 19 68 13
www.iguapop.net

Opening hours: Mon 5 pm to 9 pm, Tue–Sat 11 am to 2.30 pm and 5 pm to 9 pm
Products: Art, fashion
Public transportation: Metro Arc de Triomf, Jaume I
Map: No. 27

Cool, cooler, Iguapop—buy your zeitgeist here. The company markets young art such as graffiti, photography and video art from home and abroad. You will also find hip fashion and accessories. Music is also part of the concept: the owners have been in the promotion business for 20 years and got artists such as Nirvana, Portishead and Beck to Barcelona.

Cool, cooler, Iguapop – hier kann man Zeitgeist kaufen. Das Unternehmen vertreibt junge Kunst aus dem In- und Ausland, etwa Graffiti, Fotografien und Videokunst, außerdem hippe Mode und Accessoires. Dass auch Musik zum Konzept gehört, liegt in der Natur der Sache: Die Inhaber sind seit 20 Jahren als Promoter tätig, sie brachten schon Nirvana, Portishead und Beck nach Barcelona.

Un lieu en prise directe avec l'ère du temps, où l'on trouve une sélection d'œuvres d'art alternatif venues de tous les coins du monde – graffiti, photographies, vidéo – et, côté boutique, des vêtements et accessoires hautement tendance. La musique faisant aussi partie du concept, les propriétaires organisent des concerts depuis une vingtaine d'années et ont déjà fait venir à Barcelone des musiciens mythiques comme Nirvana, Portishead et Beck.

Cool, cooler, Iguapop: en este negocio se puede adquirir "espíritu de los tiempos", ya que comercializa arte joven nacional e internacional, como grafitis, fotografía y vídeos artísticos, además de ropa y accesorios de última moda. También la música forma parte del concepto, algo natural si se piensa que los propietarios trabajan desde hace veinte años como promotores; ellos llevaron a Barcelona a Nirvana, Portishead o Beck.

Nobodinoz

Calle Séneca, 9
08006 Barcelona
Gràcia
Phone: +34 / 93 / 3 68 63 35
www.nobodinoz.com

Opening hours: Mon–Sat 10.30 am to 8.30 pm
Products: Toys, fashion, decoration, furniture for kids
Public transportation: Metro Diagonal
Map: No. 28

To find something original for the little ones in Nobodinoz is a breeze. Furniture, apparel, toys, or home décor—you will find nothing but cool designer items in Spain's first concept store for children up to the age of ten. The boutique on Séneca Street, at the top of the Passeig de Gràcia was opened in 2006 and even boasts a stylish changing room created by French avant-garde designer Matali Crasset.

Im Nobodinoz etwas Originelles für die Kleinen zu finden ist ein Kinderspiel. Ob Möbel, Kleider, Spielzeug oder Wohndeko – in Spaniens erstem Konzept-Store für Kinder bis zehn Jahre sind alle Produkte Designerstücke. Sogar der Umkleideraum der 2006 in der Calle Séneca, oberhalb des Passeig de Gràcia eröffneten Boutique hat Stil: Er wurde von der französischen Avantgarde-Designerin Matali Crasset entworfen.

Trouver un cadeau original pour les petits est ici un jeu d'enfant. Meubles, vêtements, accessoires, jouets, décoration pour la chambre : tous les articles présentés ici ont été spécialement conçus et imaginés pour les enfants jusqu'à dix ans. Située dans la rue Séneca, en haut du Passeig de Gràcia, la boutique a ouvert ses portes en 2006. Ses cabines d'essayage sont l'œuvre de Matali Crasset, conceptrice française d'avant-garde.

Encontrar algo original para los más pequeños es un juego de niños en Nobodinoz. Ya se trate de muebles, prendas de vestir, juguetes o artículos de decoración, en este multiespacio, el primero en España dedicado a los niños menores de diez años, todos los productos son artículos de diseño. Incluso los probadores de esta boutique, abierta en 2006 en la calle Séneca, por encima del Passeig de Gràcia, tienen estilo: han sido concebidos por la diseñadora francesa vanguardista Matali Crasset.

Oriol Balaguer

Plaça de Sant Gregori Taumaturg, 2
08021 Barcelona
Sarrià Sant Gervasi
Phone: +34 / 93 / 2 01 18 46
www.oriolbalaguer.com

Opening hours: Mon–Fri 10 am to 2.30 pm and 5 pm to 9 pm, Sat 10 am to 4 pm and 5 pm to 9 pm, Sun 9 am to 2.30 pm
Products: Confectionary, chocolate, cakes and pastries
Public transportation: Bus Doctor Fleming – Avinguda Sarrià
Map: No. 29

Forget everything you think you know about chocolate—Oriol Balaguer will guide you into a different dimension. In his white, effectively illuminated boutique you will not find anything that you have seen elsewhere. This is the haute couture of desserts. Each piece by the star patissier is an abstract work of art—his confectionery collections will have your taste buds explode.

Vergessen Sie alles, was Sie über Schokolade zu wissen glauben – Oriol Balaguer entführt Sie in eine andere Dimension. In seiner weißen, effektvoll ausgeleuchteten Boutique gibt es nichts Süßes von der Stange, sondern nur Haute Couture. Die Desserts des Star-Patissiers sind abstrakte Kunstwerke, seine Konfekt-Kollektionen wahre Geschmacksfeuerwerke.

Oubliez tout ce que vous croyez savoir sur le chocolat. Oriol Balaguer vous fait entrer dans une autre dimension. Dans sa boutique blanche et abondamment illuminée, on ne trouve pas du prêt-à-porter, mais de la haute couture. Les desserts de la star des pâtissiers sont des œuvres d'art abstrait, et ses confiseries un feu d'artifice pour les papilles.

Olvídese de todo lo que creía saber hasta ahora sobre el chocolate: Oriol Balaguer le traslada a otra dimensión. En su blanca boutique, iluminada de forma efectista, no hay dulces prêt-à-porter, sólo de "alta costura". Los postres de este pastelero estrella son obras de arte abstractas; sus colecciones de bombones, auténticos fuegos de artificio de sabor.

Vila Viniteca

Carrer dels Agullers, 7
08003 Barcelona
El Born
Phone: +34 / 93 / 7 77 70 17
www.vilaviniteca.es

Opening hours: Mon–Sat 8.30 am to 8.30 pm
Products: Wine, spirits
Public transportation: Metro Jaume I, Barceloneta
Map: No. 30

Since it opened in 1932, the family-run business Vila Viniteca has turned into an institution in Barcelona. It stocks the finest wines from all over the world and a great assortment of sherry, brandy, vermouth, and other rarities—all in all some 7000 different good wines, many of which are exclusively sold here! The gourmet section across the street is ideal to taste what is on offer.

Seit 1932 ist das Familienunternehmen Vila Viniteca eine Institution in Barcelona. Es führt die köstlichsten Weine aus der ganzen Welt, außerdem eine reiche Auswahl an Sherrys, Brandys, Wermutsorten und Raritäten – insgesamt rund 7000 edle Tropfen! Viele Produkte vertreibt das Geschäft exklusiv. In der Gourmetabteilung gleich gegenüber können die Weine auch degustiert werden.

Fondée en 1932, cette affaire familiale, véritable institution à Barcelone, propose une vaste sélection de vins et de liqueurs du monde entier – sherry, brandy, vermouth et autres raretés –, en tout plus de 7000 vins différents, dont elle a l'exclusivité pour beaucoup d'entre eux ! De l'autre côté de la rue, un autre local est dédié à la dégustation des nectars proposés.

La empresa familiar Vila Viniteca es una institución en Barcelona desde 1932. Vende los vinos más exquisitos de todo el mundo, además de una amplia selección de jerez, brandy, vermut y algunas rarezas, en total alrededor de 7.000 caldos nobles. De muchos productos ostenta la comercialización en exclusiva. En su sección de gourmets, justo enfrente, se pueden degustar los vinos.

VILA VINITECA
JEAN LEON
CELLER CA
CAPÇANES
Cérvoles
ARTADI
Les Terrasses
Les Terrasses
Les Terrasses
Les Terrasses

Vinçon

Passeig de Gràcia, 96
08008 Barcelona
Eixample
Phone: +34 / 93 / 2 15 60 50
www.vincon.com

Opening hours: Mon–Sat 10 am to 8.30 pm
Products: Design furniture, furnishing accessories
Public transportation: Metro Passeig de Gràcia, Diagonal
Map: No. 31

It must be original and have cult potential, otherwise Vinçon does not stock a product. The designer store on the grand boulevard Passeig de Gràcia offers lifestyle across the board: cool furniture, smart domestic appliances, unusual accessories. And because setting trends is a total must they even have artists redesigning their bags every year.

Originell muss es sein und Kult-Potential haben, andernfalls nimmt das Vinçon ein Produkt nicht in seine Palette auf. Das Designkaufhaus am Prachtboulevard Passeig de Gràcia bietet Lifestyle auf der ganzen Linie: coole Möbel, pfiffige Haushaltsgeräte, ausgefallene Accessoires. Und weil Trendsetting hier Trumpf ist, werden sogar die Tragetaschen jedes Jahr von Künstlern neu gestaltet.

Pour faire son entrée chez Vinçon, chaque objet doit être unique et pouvoir devenir un produit culte. La boutique design du grand boulevard Passeig de Gràcia répond à de multiples envies domestiques : mobilier tendance, petit électroménager futé, accessoires originaux. Et parce que lancer des tendances est un must absolu, des artistes élaborent chaque année un nouveau design pour les sacs d'emballage.

Un producto ha de ser original y tener potencial de culto, de otro modo Vinçon no lo incluye en su surtido. Este comercio de diseño en la representativa avenida del Passeig de Gràcia ofrece lifestyle en todas sus facetas: muebles cool, coquetones utensilios de cocina, accesorios llamativos. Y como marcar la pauta es lo que cuenta, incluso las bolsas de compra presentan un diseño artístico nuevo cada año.

SHOPS . Vinçon   157

Xocoa

Carrer Vidriería, 4
08003 Barcelona
Ciutat Vella
Phone: +34 / 93 / 3 19 79 05
www.xocoa-bcn.com

Opening hours: Mon–Sat 11am to 10 pm, Sun noon to 3 pm and 4 pm to 10 pm
Products: Chocolate, pralines
Public transportation: Metro Jaume I
Map: No. 32

Russell James' Special Tip
While the chocolate bars featuring green tea or fiery Jamaican peppers are amazing, don't miss the delicious chocolate beer.

Chocoholics beware! The family-run business' hallmark is somewhat unusually flavored chocolates such as rosemary, puffed rice or green tea. And because the whole thing has to look good as well, top graphic artists design the packaging. The 15 branches in Barcelona also stock calorie-free items such as chocolate-scented shower gel.

Chocoholics aufgepasst! Markenzeichen des Familienunternehmens sind Schokoladen in ausgefallenen Geschmacksrichtungen, etwa Rosmarin, Knusperreis oder Grüner Tee. Und weil das Auge mitisst, werden die Verpackungen von Top-Grafikern entworfen. Die 15 Filialen in Barcelona haben aber auch Kalorienfreies im Sortiment, zum Beispiel Duschgel mit Schokoduft.

Accros du chocolat, attention danger ! On trouvera dans cette entreprise familiale des chocolats aux saveurs étonnantes : romarin, riz soufflé ou encore thé vert. Et parce qu'en matière de chocolat, le style compte aussi, la conception des emballages a été confiée à des artistes et graphistes de renom. Les 15 boutiques barcelonaises proposent également des articles non caloriques, notamment un gel douche parfumé au chocolat.

¡Ojo con los adictos al chocolate! Este negocio familiar está especializado en chocolates de sabores insólitos, como romero, arroz inflado o té verde. Y como la presentación es decisiva, los envoltorios están diseñados por grafistas consagrados. Las 15 filiales de Barcelona disponen también de un surtido "bajo en calorías" que incluye, por ejemplo, jabón de ducha con aroma de chocolate.

HIGHLIGHTS

Casa Batlló

Passeig de Gràcia, 43
08007 Barcelona
Eixample
Phone: +34 / 93 / 2 16 03 06
www.casabatllo.cat

Opening hours: Daily from 9 am to 8 pm
Public transportation: Metro Passeig de Gràcia
Map: No. 34

The Casa Batlló, converted by Antoni Gaudí for a captain of industry in 1906, is literally fabulous: the design was inspired by the dragon of the legend surrounding St. George, Catalonia's patron saint. The balustrades represent the skulls of his victims, the facade glitters like his scales, and the roof is shaped like his arched back. Since 2005, Casa Batlló is listed as a UNESCO World Heritage site.

Im wahrsten Sinne sagenhaft ist die 1906 von Antoni Gaudí für einen Industriellen umgebaute Casa Batlló: Inspiration für das Design war der Drache aus der Legende des Heiligen Georg, Schutzpatron Kataloniens. Die Balkonbrüstungen sehen aus wie die Schädel seiner Opfer, die Außenwand schillert bunt wie seine Schuppenhaut, das Dach hat die Form seines Rückenpanzers. Seit 2005 gehört Casa Batlló zum Weltkulturerbe der UNESCO.

Remodelée en 1906 par Antoni Gaudí pour le compte d'un industriel, la Casa Batlló est littéralement fabuleuse, puisque l'architecte s'est inspiré du dragon de la légende de saint Georges, patron de la Catalogne. Les balcons évoquent les crânes de ses victimes, la façade scintille comme ses écailles, le toit a la forme de la carapace de son dos. Depuis 2005, elle est inscrite au Patrimoine mondial de l'UNESCO.

La Casa Batlló, reconstruida en 1906 por Antoni Gaudí para un industrial, es legendaria en el sentido más auténtico, ya que su diseño está inspirado en el dragón de la leyenda de san Jordi, el patrón de Cataluña: los pretiles de los balcones parecen calaveras de sus víctimas, la fachada es irisada como su piel escamosa, el tejado semeja su coraza dorsal. Desde el año 2005, la Casa Batlló forma parte del Patrimonio de la Humanidad de la UNESCO.

Caixa Forum

Avinguda del Marquès de Comillas, 6–8
08038 Barcelona
Sants-Montjuïc
Phone: +34 / 93 / 4 76 86 00
www.fundacio.lacaixa.es

Opening hours: Mon–Sun 10 am to 8 pm, Sat 10 am to 10 pm
Public transportation: Metro, bus España, Avinguda Marquès de Comillas
Map: No. 33

The art nouveau building which once was home to a clothing factory is worth a visit in its own right. To-day the Caixa Forum is one of Barcelona's liveliest and most active cultural locations. The cultural and social center hosts concerts and readings as well as exhibitions on artists such as Dalí, Rodin, Freud, Turner, and Hogarth.

Allein das Jugendstil-Gebäude, das früher eine Textilfabrik beherbergte, ist schon einen Besuch wert. Heute ist das Caixa Forum einer der lebendigsten und aktivsten kulturellen Orte der Stadt. Die kulturelle und soziale Begegnungsstätte bietet neben Konzerten und Lesungen auch sehenswerten Ausstellungen Raum, die sich Künstlern wie Dalí, Rodin, Freud, Turner und Hogarth widmen.

Cet immeuble art nouveau, qui abritait autrefois une usine textile, mérite une visite. Aujourd'hui, la Caixa Forum est l'un des lieux culturels les plus dynamiques de Barcelone. On assiste ici à des concerts, à des conférences, mais aussi à des expositions consacrées à Dalí, Rodin, Freud, Turner, ou encore Hogarth.

Ya sólo su edificio modernista, que en el pasado albergó una fábrica textil, es merecedor de una visita. Caixa Forum es hoy por hoy uno de los espacios culturales más vivos y activos de la ciudad. Este centro cultural y social, además de ofrecer conciertos y lecturas, cuenta con un valioso espacio expositivo dedicado a artistas como Dalí, Rodin, Freud, Turner y Hogarth.

Obra Social "la Caixa"

Benvinguts
Bienvenidos
Benvidos
Ongi etorri
Welcome
أهلاً وسهلاً
Bienvenue
Willkommen
歡迎光臨

Gran Teatre del Liceu

La Rambla, 51–59
08002 Barcelona
Ciutat Vella
Phone: +34 / 93 / 3 06 41 00
www.liceubarcelona.com

Opening hours: Guided tours of the public areas Mon–Sun from 10 am, unguided tours of the public areas Mon–Sun 11.30 am, noon, 12.30 pm and 1 pm
Ticket service: +34 / 90 / 2 53 33 53, www.servicaixa.com
Public transportation: Metro Liceu
Map: No. 35

The Gran Teatre del Liceu is one of Europe's most beautiful and magnificent opera houses—and with good reason! The house was completely renovated after a fire in 1994 and its opulent décor is simply captivating. Modern technology, superb acoustics and the superlative ambiance enthuse each and every opera lover.

Das Gran Teatre del Liceu zählt zu den schönsten und prächtigsten Opernhäusern Europas – und das zu Recht! Das Haus, das nach einem Brand im Jahr 1994 komplett renoviert wurde, besticht vor allem durch eine opulente Ausstattung. Die moderne Technik, die ausgezeichnete Akustik und das unübertreffliche Ambiente begeistern jeden Opernliebhaber.

Le Gran Teatre del Liceu est l'une des plus belles salles d'opéra d'Europe. À juste titre ! Entièrement rénovée à la suite d'un incendie en 1994, elle offre un décor aussi opulent que captivant. Sa technologie moderne, son acoustique hors norme et son atmosphère inégalable raviront les amoureux de l'opéra.

El Gran Teatre del Liceu se cuenta entre los teatros operísticos de época más bellos y soberbios de Europa, y con razón: el edificio, que tras un incendio en 1994 fue renovado por completo, llama la atención sobre todo por su opulenta decoración. Su moderna técnica, su excelente acústica y su insuperable ambiente entusiasman a todos los amantes de la ópera.

Jardí Botànic de Barcelona

Carrer del Dr. Font i Quer, 2
Parc de Montjuïc
08038 Barcelona
Sants-Montjuïc
Phone: +34 / 93 / 4 26 49 35
www.jardibotanic.bcn.cat

Opening hours: April, May and Sept daily 10 am to 7 pm, June, July and Aug daily 10 am to 8 pm, Nov, Dec and Jan daily 10 am to 5 pm, Feb, March and Oct daily 10 am to 6 pm, closed on Dec 25th and Jan 1st
Public transportation: Bus Parc de Montjuïc   **Map:** No. 36

Eva Padberg's Special Tip
This lush, tranquil garden is a great spot to spend an afternoon unwinding and soaking up some sunlight.

Arrive, switch off, and breathe again! The botanical gardens located high above the city on the Montjuïc are an oasis of peace and quiet—and a small sensation: you can travel around the world's flora on the 37-acres site. A collection of Mediterranean climate plants from Africa, Australia, Chile, California, the Canary Islands, and the Mediterranean await you.

Ankommen, abschalten, aufatmen! Der hoch über der Stadt auf dem Montjuïc gelegene botanische Garten ist eine Oase der Ruhe – und eine kleine Sensation: Auf 14 Hektar kann man einmal um die Erde reisen und die Pflanzenwelten verschiedener Kontinente bestaunen. Die mediterrane Flora Afrikas, Australiens, Chiles, Kaliforniens, der Kanaren und des Mittelmeerraums findet sich hier.

Dès l'arrivée ici, on respire ! Les jardins botaniques, situés en surplomb de la ville sur le promontoire de Montjuïc, sont une oasis de calme. Et on y voyage : dans ce parc de 14 hectares, vous ferez le tour du monde de la flore et découvrirez des plantes d'Afrique, d'Australie, du Chili, de Californie, des Canaries et du bassin méditerranéen.

¡Llegar, desconectar, respirar! El Jardín Botánico, situado por encima del nivel de la ciudad en el monte Montjuïc, es un oasis de tranquilidad… y una pequeña sensación. En sus 14 hectáreas se puede realizar un viaje alrededor del mundo y admirar la flora de los distintos continentes. El jardín reúne especies africanas, australianas, de Chile, California, las Canarias y del ámbito mediterráneo.

Museu d'Art Contemporani de Barcelona – MACBA

Plaça dels Àngels, 1
08001 Barcelona
El Raval
Phone: +34 / 93 / 4 12 08 10
www.macba.cat

Opening hours: 25th Sept to 23rd June Mon-Fri 11 am to 7.30 pm, Sat 10 am to 8 pm, Sun and legal holidays 10 am to 3 pm, 24th June to 24th Sept Mon–Fri 11 am to 8 pm, Thu and Fri 11 am to midnight, Sat 10 am to 8 pm, Sun and legal holidays 10 am to 3 pm
Closed: Tuesdays (except holidays), December 25th and January 1st
Public transportation: Metro, bus Catalunya and Universitat
Map: No. 37

The façade is gleaming white with clear, strong lines: the museum for modern art by the American architect Richard Meier is its own biggest exhibit. Opened in 1995, it is famous for its provocative exhibitions. The MACBA Collection consists of many works from Catalonian, Spanish and International artists and gives an overview of the fundamental aspects of Contemporary Art.

Strahlend weiß die Fassade, klar und streng die Linienführung: Das vom amerikanischen Architekten Richard Meier entworfene Museum für moderne Kunst ist selbst sein größtes Exponat. 1995 eröffnet, ist es bekannt für seine provokanten Ausstellungen. Die MACBA Kollektion besteht aus Arbeiten von katalanischen, spanischen sowie internationalen Künstlern und gibt einen Überblick über die wesentlichen Aspekte zeitgenössischer Kunst.

Avec sa façade d'un blanc étincelant et ses lignes nettes et épurées, le musée d'art moderne, conçu par l'architecte américain Richard Meier, vaut à lui seul le déplacement. Depuis son ouverture en 1995, il se distingue aussi par le caractère provoquant de ses expositions. La collection du MACBA, constituée d'œuvres d'artistes catalans, espagnols et internationaux, donne un aperçu des grandes tendances de l'art contemporain.

Fachadas de blanco resplandeciente, líneas puras y austeras: este museo de arte contemporáneo, diseñado por Richard Meier, es él mismo una pieza de exposición. Inaugurado en 1995, es célebre por sus provocadoras exposiciones. La colección del MACBA está integrada por trabajos de artistas catalanes, españoles e internacionales, y ofrece una panorámica de los aspectos esenciales del arte contemporáneo.

Mercat de la Boqueria

La Rambla, 89
08002 Barcelona
Ciutat Vella
Phone: +34 / 93 / 3 18 25 84
www.boqueria.info

Opening hours: Mon–Sat 8 am to 8.30 pm
Products: Fruits, vegetables, fish, meat, sweets
Public transportation: Metro Liceu
Map: No. 38

Eva Padberg's Special Tip
Sprawling and chaotic, this centuries-old market sells everything from verdant fruits and vegetables to ocean-fresh fish.

Here you will see Barcelona's top chefs on the prowl: there is no fresh product that cannot be had in the city's most famous grocery market. A walk through it equals to a festival of the senses with a multitude of colors wherever you cast your eye, not to mention the aroma of all the delicacies! The steel roof decorated with glass mosaics was completed in 1914 but the market itself dates back more than 300 years.

Hier gehen die Starköche der Stadt auf Streifzug: Kein frisches Produkt, das der berühmteste Lebens-mittelmarkt Barcelonas nicht zu bieten hat. Jeder Rundgang ist ein Fest für die Sinne. Wo man hin-schaut, ein Feuerwerk an Farben und erst der Duft all der Delikatessen! Das mit Glasmosaiken verzierte Stahldach wurde 1914 eingeweiht, die Anfänge des Marktes reichen aber mehr als 300 Jahre zurück.

Tous les grands chefs de Barcelone y font leurs courses. Il est vrai qu'il n'existe pas de produit frais que l'on ne puisse se procurer sur le marché le plus renommé de la ville. Le simple fait de s'y promener est un véritable festival de sensations. Partout où se porte le regard, c'est un feu d'artifice de couleurs et d'arômes ! Le toit en acier décoré de mosaïques de verre date de 1914, mais le marché lui-même existe depuis plus de trois siècles.

Es el lugar donde los chefs de cocina más célebres de la ciudad llevan a cabo sus "correrías": no hay producto fresco que no se encuentre en este famoso mercado de Barcelona. Cada recorrido es una fiesta para los sentidos. Allí donde se posa la mirada estalla un fuego de artificio de colores –por no mencionar los aromas– de todos los manjares. El tejado de acero decorado con vidrieras se concluyó en 1914, pero los orígenes del mercado se remontan a hace más de 300 años.

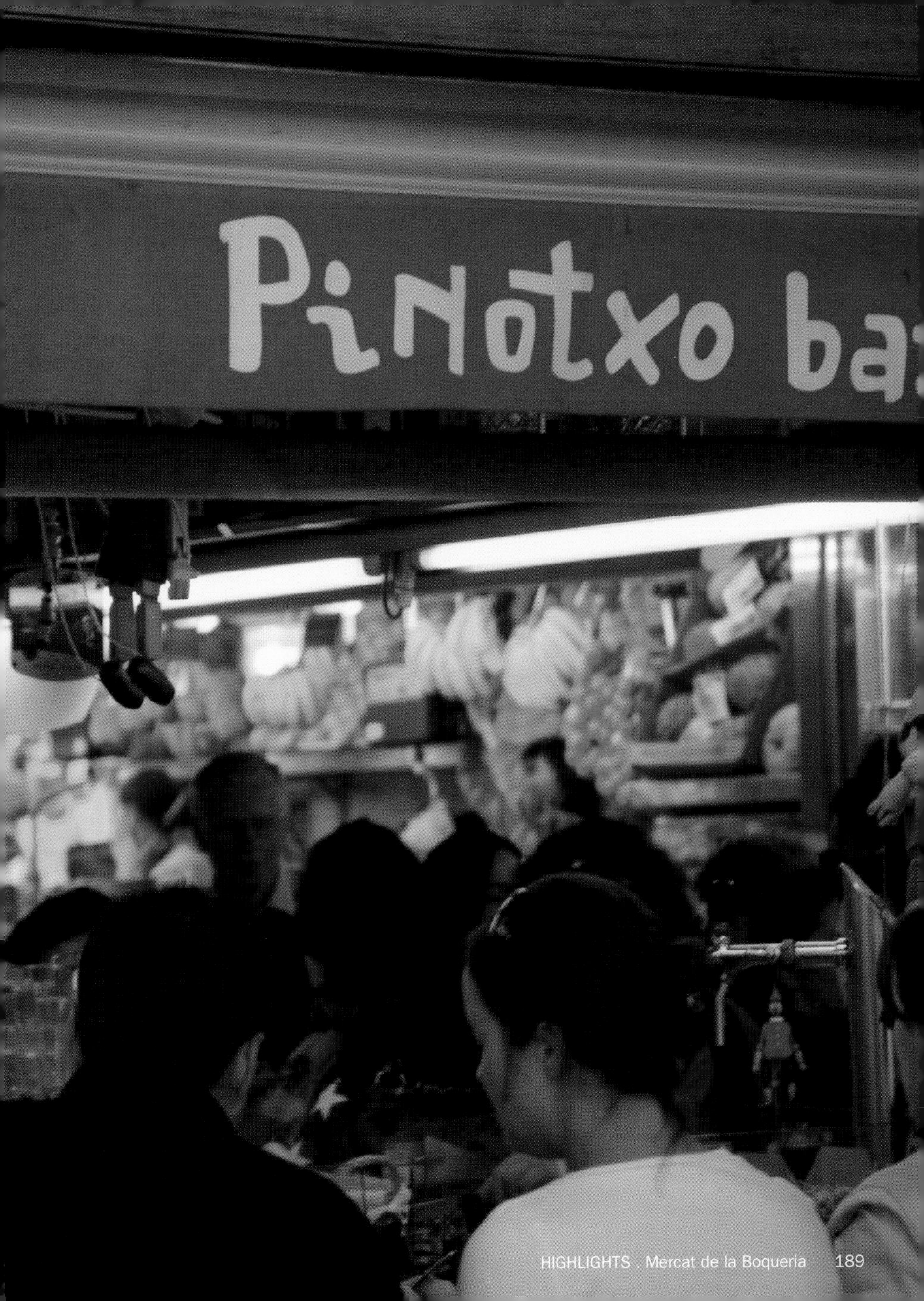
Pinotxo ba

PAÍS
22'99
€/kg

CAMARÓN
GALLEGO
30'99

NAVAJA·VIVA
SIN ARENA
17'€
99

PAÍS
22'99
€/kg

CAMARÓN
GALLEGO
30€

VIEIRA·VIVA
GALLEGA
14'€
99

Platja de la Barceloneta

Ciutat Vella

Public transportation: Metro Barceloneta
Map: No. 39

Beach boys and Baywatch—that is also a part of Barcelona. Three miles of beach over six bays invite one to sunbathe or go swimming in the waves. Barcelona's favorite beach is the 1200-yards long Platja de la Barceloneta, named after the neighborhood it borders on. The beach's landmark is the sculpture by Rebecca Horn. During the winter months it is a hot spot for surfers.

Beachboys und Baywatch – auch das ist Barcelona. Fünf Kilometer Strand in sechs aufeinanderfolgenden Buchten laden zum Sonnenbaden und Schwimmen ein. Beliebtester Strand ist die 1100 Meter lange Platja de la Barceloneta im gleichnamigen Stadtteil, Wahrzeichen ist die Skulptur von Rebecca Horn. Während der Wintermonate ist der Strand übrigens Hotspot für Surfer.

Barcelone, c'est aussi la mer. Ses cinq kilomètres de plage et ses six baies sont irrésistibles pour qui aime se baigner et lézarder au soleil. S'étirant sur 1 100 mètres, la Platja de la Barceloneta, du nom du quartier voisin, est particulièrement appréciée. On reconnaît les lieux à la statue de Rebecca Horn. Pendant les mois d'hiver, c'est le paradis des surfer.

Barcelona también cuenta con sus *beachboys* y *baywatch*. Cinco quilómetros de playa en seis bahías consecutivas invitan a nadar y a los baños de sol. La playa más popular es la Platja de la Barceloneta, en el barrio del mismo nombre. La playa tiene 1.100 metros de longitud y un símbolo emblemático: una escultura de Rebecca Horn. Durante los meses de invierno, es lugar de cita ineludible de los surfistas.

Les Rambles

08002 Barcelona
Ciutat Vella

Public transportation: Metro Drassanes, Liceu, Catalunya
Map: No. 40

Russell James' Special Tip

Instead of strolling down this tree-lined pedestrian mall, sit at one of the countless cafes, sip a fruity sangria and watch the action pass by.

A street is a street is a street. Or is it? Not this one! The 1.2-mile long Les Rambles connects the Plaça de Catalunya with the port and forms the pulsating heart of this city. Big plane trees and beautiful buildings in the modernist style line the famous promenade with intermittent cafés, souvenir shops and flower stands. Street musicians and artists turn it into a large open air stage.

Eine Straße ist eine Straße ist eine Straße? Nicht diese! Die zwei Kilometer langen Les Rambles, die die Plaça de Catalunya mit dem Hafen verbinden, sind das pulsierende Herz der Stadt. Große Platanen und prachtvolle Modernisme-Bauten säumen die berühmte Promenade, Cafés, Souvenirgeschäfte und Blumenstände flankieren sie, Straßenkünstler und Musiker machen sie zu einer großen Kleinkunstbühne.

Rien ne ressemble plus à une rue qu'une autre rue, direz-vous. Pas celle-ci ! Sur deux kilomètres, les Rambles, qui relient la Plaça de Catalunya au port, constituent le cœur battant de la ville. Des platanes imposants et de somptueux immeubles modernistes bordent la promenade qui offre également des cafés, des boutiques de souvenirs et des étals de fleurs. Musiciens de rue et artistes font de cette avenue une immense scène en plein air.

¿Una calle es una calle es una calle? ¡Ésta no! El bulevar de Las Ramblas, que comunica la Plaça de Catalunya con el puerto a lo largo de dos kilómetros, constituye la médula de la ciudad. Enormes plátanos y espléndidos edificios modernistas orlan esta famosa avenida; cafeterías, tiendas de suvenires y puestos de flores la flanquean; artistas callejeros y músicos la convierten cada día en un gran escenario de variedades.

Sagrada Família

Carrer de Mallorca, 401
08013 Barcelona
Eixample
Phone: +34 / 93 / 2 07 30 31
www.sagradafamilia.org

Opening hours: Oct–March 9 am to 6 pm, April–Sept 9 am to 8 pm
Public transportation: Metro Sagrada Família
Map: No. 41

This is Spain's biggest tourist attraction and probably the world's most famous building site: work on the monumental cathedral has not stopped since 1882. The slender spires and fanciful ornaments bear the hallmarks of Antoni Gaudí, who spent more than 40 years of his life on this building. The mammoth project is financed exclusively through donations and entrance fees.

Sie ist die größte Touristenattraktion Spaniens und die wohl berühmteste Baustelle der Welt: Seit 1882 wird an der monumentalen Kathedrale gearbeitet. Die schlanken Türme und die phantasievolle Ornamentierung tragen die Handschrift Antoni Gaudís, der seinem Lebenswerk mehr als 40 Jahre widmete. Finanziert wird das Mammutprojekt seit Baubeginn allein durch Spenden und Eintrittsgelder.

C'est la plus grande attraction touristique d'Espagne, et probablement le chantier le plus célèbre du monde : le début des travaux de construction de la monumentale cathédrale remonte à 1882. Les flèches élancées et les étranges ornements portent la signature d'Antoni Gaudí, qui consacra plus de 40 ans de sa vie à ce projet gigantesque financé exclusivement, depuis le début, par des dons et la recette des entrées.

Es una de las mayores atracciones turísticas de España y, posiblemente, el edificio en obras más famoso del mundo: esta monumental catedral está en construcción desde 1882. Sus esbeltas torres y ornamentación de gran fantasía llevan la firma de Antoni Gaudí, quien consagró a su obra más de cuarenta años. El monumental proyecto se ha financiado desde sus comienzos únicamente mediante donaciones y la recaudación de las entradas.

Torre Agbar

Plaça de les Glòries Catalanes / Avinguda Diagonal, 211
08018 Barcelona
Sant Martí
www.torreagbar.com

Public transportation: Metro Glòries
Map: No. 42

Russell James' Special Tip

For a cheap and romantic date, bring your sweetheart to the tower after sunset and watch the dazzling—and free—nocturnal illumination.

It is not without reason that the 466-feet tall high-tech tower resembles an erupting geyser in both shape and color. The design by French architect Jean Nouvel was inspired by the client, the municipal water authorities. 40 different colors on the shell create ever-changing light effects. Especially at night, the monster made of glass and aluminum with its 4500 lighted windows turns into a dazzling chameleon.

Dass der 142 Meter hohe Hightechturm in Form und Farbe einem Geysir ähnelt, dessen Fontäne aus dem Boden schießt, hat seinen Grund: Das Design des französischen Architekten Jean Nouvel ist eine Referenz an den Bauherrn, die städtischen Wasserwerke. 40 verschiedene Lackfarben auf der Oberfläche zaubern changierende Lichteffekte und besonders nachts wird der Glas-Aluminium-Koloss durch die 4500 beleuchteten Fenster zu einem schillernden Chamäleon.

Ce n'est pas par hasard si cette tour high-tech de 142 mètres de haut évoque un geyser, par sa forme et sa couleur. Ce sont les Eaux de Barcelone (Aguas de Barcelona), entreprise municipale actuellement locataire du lieu, qui ont inspiré l'architecte français Jean Nouvel. Constituée de 40 couleurs différentes, l'enveloppe externe produit d'extraordinaires effets de lumière. La nuit, le monstre de verre et d'aluminium, avec ses 4 500 fenêtres éclairées, se transforme en un étincelant caméléon.

Que esta torre de alta tecnología de 142 metros de altura recuerde, tanto por su forma como por su color, un géiser con el chorro de agua surgiendo desde el suelo tiene su razón de ser: el diseño del arquitecto francés Jean Nouvel alude a los propietarios, una empresa de aguas municipales. El lacado de la superficie en cuarenta tonos distintos crea efectos lumínicos cambiantes y, en particular durante la noche, este coloso de cristal y aluminio se transforma en un camaleón mutante gracias a sus 4.500 ventanas iluminadas.

Transbordador Aeri del Port

Passeig de Joan de Borbó, 88
Torre de Sant Sebastià
08003 Barcelona
Ciutat Vella
Phone: +34 / 93 / 4 30 47 16

Opening hours: Jan–Feb daily 10.30 am to 5.45 pm, March–10th June 10.45 am to 7 pm, 11th June–16th Sept 11 am to 8 pm, 17th Sept–21st Oct 10.45 am to 7 pm, 22nd Oct–31st Dec 10.30 am to 5.45 pm
Prices: Single ticket € 9, return € 12.50
Public transportation: Metro Barceloneta (Torre de Sant Sebastià)
Map: No. 43

The ride in the lift to the top of the 255-feet tall Torre Sant Sebastià tower on the Platja de la Barceloneta is a spectacle in its own right. This can only be topped by sitting in a red cable car and floating the 1,586 yards up to Montjuïc while looking down at the massive port—high-altitude euphoria is guaranteed! The 351-feet tall Torre Jaume I support tower is the second tallest cable car support structure in the world.

Schon die Fahrt mit dem Lift auf den 78 Meter hohen Turm Torre Sant Sebastià an der Platja de la Barceloneta ist ein Spektakel. Von dort schwebt man dann in der roten Gondel auf 1450 Metern Länge quer über die riesige Hafenanlage hinauf auf den Montjuïc, Höhenrausch garantiert! Gestützt wird die Drahtseilbahn vom 107 Meter hohen Torre Jaume I, übrigens die zweithöchste Seilbahnstütze der Welt.

Le simple fait de prendre l'ascenseur qui conduit au sommet de la Torre Sant Sebastià, à 78 mètres d'altitude sur la Platja de la Barceloneta, est un spectacle à part entière. Mais une fois à bord de la cabine rouge, on vit un grand moment en « survolant » l'immense port sur 1 450 mètres, jusqu'au promontoire de Montjuïc. Griserie garantie ! Culminant à 107 mètres, la Torre Jaume I est le deuxième pylône de téléphérique le plus haut du monde.

Ya sólo el viaje con el telesilla hasta la Torre Sant Sebastià, de 78 metros de altura, en la Platja de la Barceloneta es todo un espectáculo. Desde allí, se avanza en cabinas rojas a lo largo de 1.450 metros a través de la gigantesca área del puerto en dirección a la montaña de Montjuïc: ¡la euforia de las alturas está garantizada! La Torre Jaume I, de 107 metros de altitud, que sirve de soporte al transbordador es el segundo pilar de teleférico más alto del mundo.

ARRIVAL IN BARCELONA

By Plane

Aeroport de Barcelona (BCN) – El Prat

Phone: +34 / 90 / 2 40 47 04

www.barcelona-airport.com

Barcelona's international main airport is located in El Prat de Llobregat, about 10 km (6 miles) southwest from the center of town. There are trains departing from the airport every 30 mins (from Spain's national railway operator Renfe) that are going to the railway stations Sants, Passeig de Gràcia and the Estació de França (traveling time: approx. 30 mins). There is also an airport bus called Aerobús A1 that departs every 10 mins with destination Plaça de Catalunya in the center of Barcelona. You will find information signs for the Aerobús at the airport. Taking a cab is another option. It takes 25 to 30 mins and costs approx. 25 €.

Aeroport de Girona (GRO)

Phone: +34 / 97 / 2 18 66 06

www.girona-airport.net

The Girona airport, situated about 100 km (62 miles) northeast of Barcelona, is mainly frequented by low-budget airlines. Buses depart regularly from the terminal and will bring you to the Girona railway station (Estació de Girona). From there it is another 30 mins to Barcelona by express train which amounts to a total traveling time of 1 1/4 hours. It is also possible to go directly from the airport to the main bus station in Barcelona (Estació d'Autobusos Barcelona North) taking the Barcelona Bus (traveling time: 1 1/4 hours, single ticket 12 €, Phone: +34 / 90 / 2 36 15 50). From the bus station it is just a 5–10 mins walk to the subway.

Aeroport de Reus (REU)

Phone: +34 / 90 / 2 40 47 04

www.reus-airport.net

The Reus airport is situated about 110 km (68 miles) southwest of Barcelona. The bus company Hispano Igualadina is covering the route between the airport and the city of Barcelona (María Cristina square and Sants station, single ticket 12 €).The journey takes around 1 hour and 20 minutes and the buses can be caught directly outside of the terminal. The timetables do vary throughout the year as the journeys are planned to meet the flights that are arriving each day. For information on the route and current timetable visit www.igualadina.com or call +34 / 90 / 2 44 77 26.

By Train

Estació Central de Sants

Plaça dels Països Catalans

The main railway station is very well connected with Barcelona's subway and bus networks.

Railway Information

Renfe, Phone: +34 / 90 / 2 24 02 02 (information and tickets), Phone: +34 / 90 / 2 24 34 02 (international information), www.renfe.es

Immigration and Customs Regulations

European citizens need a valid identity card for traveling to Spain. For EU citizens there are virtually no custom regulations. Every person at the age of 17 or older is allowed to carry goods for personal needs duty-free, e.g. 800 cigarettes, 400 cigarillos, 200 cigars, 1 kg of tobacco, 10 l of liquor, 90 l of wine and 110 l of beer.

INFORMATION

Tourist Information

Spanish Tourist Office

www.tourspain.es

Turisme de Barcelona

www.barcelonaturisme.com
info@barcelonaturisme.com
Phone: +34 / 93 / 2 85 38 34
Phone: +34 / 93 / 2 85 38 33 (hotel reservation)
Fax: +34 / 93 / 2 85 38 31
Service Mon–Fri, 9 am to 8 pm

The Spanish **tourist information centers** offer abundant information materials, help finding suitable accommodation, organize city tours etc.:

Plaça de Catalunya 17-S, ground floor, daily 9 am to 9 pm
Plaça de Sant Jaume, Ciutat 2 (in the City Hall), Mon–Fri 9 am to 8 pm, Sat 10 am to 8 pm, Sun 10 am to 2 pm
Estació Central de Sants, in the central station, June–Sept daily 8 am to 8 pm, Oct–May Mon–Fri 8 am to 8 pm, Sat and Sun 8 am to 2 pm
Barcelona Airport, Terminal A and B, daily 9 am to 9 pm

Information Booths from Turisme de Barcelona:

Plaça d'Espanya, Corner Av. Reina María Cristina, July–Sept daily 10 am to 8 pm, Oct–June daily 10 am to 4 pm
Plaça de la Sagrada Família, July–Sept daily 10 am to 8 pm, Oct–June daily 10 am to 4 pm
Plaça del Portal de la Pau, at the Christopher Columbus monument, May–Oct daily 9 am to 8.30 pm, Nov–April daily 10 am to 6.30 pm

City Magazines

The small format program guide **Guía del Ocio** is published every Thu and informs its readers in Spanish about what's hot and what's not (available at newspaper stands and in tourist information centers).

The Metropolitan is an event guide in English that is published once a month and can be found in movie theatres and bars. Information about fashion, design, architecture, bars, restaurants and nightlife in English and Spanish are offered by the quarterly **b-guided**.

Websites

General

www.barcelonaturisme.com – Official website of the city's tourist office offering hotel reservation, event calendar, information about sightseeing, public transportation, guided city tours etc. (in CA, ES, EN, FR)
www.bcn.es – Very informative web service provided by Barcelona's city administration (CA, ES, EN)
www.barcelona-tourist-guide.com – Up-to-date information service and interactive city map including photo guide. Among other things: accommodation service, city guides, transportation, restaurants, weather forecast (EN)

Going Out

www.atiza.com – Concerts, bars, discos (ES)
www.guiadelocio.com/barcelona – Internet portal of the event guide Guía del Ocio offering tips for theater, concerts, movies, restaurants, bars, clubs (ES)

Art & Culture

www.bcn.es/icub – Information about cultural life in Barcelona including current programs for movie theaters and festivals (CA)
www.museupicasso.bcn.es – Website of the Picasso Museum (CA, ES, EN)
www.palaumusica.org – Opera and concert events in the Palau de la Música Catalana (CA, ES, EN)
www.tnc.es – Program of the Teatre Nacional de Catalunya (CA)

Sports & Leisure

www.basenautica.org – Sailing school and boat rental (CA)

www.circuitcat.com – Information and tickets for the F1 racetrack Circuit de Catalunya (CA, ES, EN, FR)

www.fcbarcelona.com – Website of the Barcelona-based soccer team Barça (CA, ES, EN)

Accomodation

www.barcelonaturisme.com – Online booking center of the city's tourist office (CA, ES, EN, FR)

www.oh-barcelona.com – Wide selection of apartments as well as single rooms in host families and flat-sharing communities (ES, EN, FR, D, IT)

www.citysiesta.com – Short-term accommodation, private rooms and apartments (ES, EN, FR, D, NL)

Event Calendar

www.guiadelocio.com/barcelona – Online version of the popular city guide (ES)

www.lecool.com – Online calendar informing about exhibitions, concerts, cinema and the music scene; updated once a week (ES, EN)

www.agendabcn.com – Concerts, theater, sport events etc. (CA, ES)

RECOMMENDED LITERATURE

Eduardo Mendoza

The City of Marvels. This is the story of a boy that comes from a Spanish rural area and makes his way to the top becoming the mightiest man in Barcelona.

Manuel Vázquez Montalbán

An Olympic Death. Detective story set in Barcelona right before the Olympic Games in 1992. One of the most brilliant and thrilling novels about the grumpy private detective Pepe Carvalho.

Colm Tóibín

Homage to Barcelona. A city guide with a literature like feel to it.

Carlos Ruiz Zafón

The Shadow of the Wind. Daniel Sempere grows up in the grey world of the post-civil war under the dictatorship of Franco. A mysterious book leads him into a labyrinth of adventurously interconnected life stories. This book has been in the Spanish bestseller lists for three years.

CITY TOURS

Sightseeing Tours by Bus

Bus Turístic

Open double-decker buses circulate on three different routes in the city. Starting at 9 am they depart every 5 mins during summer and every 25 mins during winter from Plaça de Catalunya, with possibility to hop on/hop off on one of the 44 stops. Tickets can be purchased in the bus or at Turisme de Barcelona; a day ticket is 21 €, a two-day ticket is 27 €.

Barcelona by Night

Julià Travel and Pullmantur Bustour will take you on a trip through Barcelona by night which includes going to a Tapas bar and a Flamenco show, Thu–Sat, 7.30 pm to approx. 12.30 am; approx. 90 €/pers.

Julià Travel, Ronda Universitat, 5
Phone: +34 / 93 / 3 17 64 54
www.juliatravel.com

Pullmantur, Gran Via, 645
Phone: +34 / 93 / 3 18 02 41
www.pullmantur-spain.com

Boat Tours

Golondrinas

Offered tours are: harbor tour, from the harbor through Port Vell to the modern industry harbor as well as from the harbor to the Port Olímpic. The piers are located at the Portal de la Pau near the Christopher Columbus monument at the end of the Rambles. April–June Mon–Sat 11 am to 6 pm, Sun 11.45 am to 7 pm, July–Sept daily 11.45 am to 7.30 pm, Oct–March Mon–Fri 11.45 am to 4 pm, Sun 11.45 am to 6 pm; duration: 30 mins – 1 1/2 hour; from 6 €/pers.; www.lasgolondrinas.com.

Guided City Tours

Private City Guides

Barcelona Guide Bureau
Via Laietana 54, Phone: +34 / 93 / 2 68 24 22
www.bgb.es
4 hours, 150–180 € (more expensive on Sat/Sun)

Thematic Tours

Starting from the Plaça de Catalunya, Turisme de Barcelona offers five different walking tours to the most important sights of the city all over the year:
Barri Gòtic, Mon–Sun 10 am (EN), Sat 12 am (CA, ES), duration: 2 hours, 12 €/pers.
Picasso, Tue, Thu and Sat 4 pm (EN), Sat 4 pm (CA, ES), duration: 2 hours 18 €/pers. (including entrance for the Picasso Museum)
Modernisme, Fri and Sat 4 pm (EN), Sat 4 pm (CA, ES), June–Sept starting at 6 pm, duration: 2 hours, 12 €/pers.
Gourmet, Fri and Sat 10.30 am (EN), Sat 10.30 am (CA, ES), duration: 2 hours, 18 €/pers.
Marina, Fri and Sat 10 am (EN), Sat 10 am (CA, ES), duration: 1 1/2 hours, 15 €/pers.

Ruta del Modernisme

The **Modernisme Center** offers a walking tour from the Palau Güell to the Catalan Art Nouveau buildings. To take the tour, purchase a copy of the Modernisme Route guidebook (12 €) which includes discounts of up to 50% on the admission charge to all the Modernista monuments in the city.
Information: Modernisme Center, Barcelona Tourist Information Center, Pl. Catalunya, 17, basement, Phone: +34 / 93 / 3 17 76 52

Lookouts

El Corte Inglés

Plaça de Catalunya
From the cafeteria in the upper floor of this department store you have a wonderful view over the Eixample district, Mon–Sat 10 am to 10 pm.

Mirador de Colom

Plaça del Portal de la Pau
The viewing platform (60 m / 200 ft high) of the Christopher Columbus monument offers a fantastic view over the harbor, the Rambles and the old city. Elevator costs 2.50 €/pers.

Montjuïc

Using the cable car Transbordador Aeri you can go from the Torre de Sant Sebastià in Barceloneta to the lookout at the Plaça de l'Armada on Barcelona's trademark mountain Montjuïc. From there you have an incredible view over the harbor and the city center. Cable car daily 11 am to 5.30 pm (these times vary), every 15 mins; one-way tickets cost 9 €.

Sagrada Família

www.sagradafamilia.org

The elevator takes you to the spires of the cathedral (55 m / 180 ft and 65 m / 210 ft high). April–Sept 9 am to 8 pm, Oct–March 9 am to 6 pm; 2.50 €/pers.

Torre de Collserola

Carretera de Vallvidrera al Tibidabo
www.torredecollserola.com
The radio tower on the Tibidabo is 288 m / 945 ft high and has a glazed lookout platform in 115 m / 377 ft height. Wed–Sun 11 am to 2.30 pm, 3.30 pm to 7 pm; 5.50 €/pers.

TICKETS AND DISCOUNTS

Ticket Offices

Servi-Caixa

Phone: +34 / 90 / 2 33 22 11
www.servicaixa.com
Servi-Caixa sells tickets for cultural as well as for sport events. The tickets can be purchased at the cash machines in La Caixa banks.

Institut de Cultura de Barcelona

Rambles 99, in the Palau de la Virreina
Phone: +34 / 93 / 3 01 77 75

Discounts

Barcelona Card

This card offers free transportation with bus and subway as well as reduced fares for the Aerobús from/to the airport, free entrance in twelve selected museums and entrance discounts of 10–50% in other museums, theatres, leisure facilities, restaurants, nightclubs and shops. It is available at the city's tourist information centers or online at www.barcelonaturisme.com. The card is valid for 2, 3, 4 or 5 days and its price depends on duration of validity (24–38 €/pers.).

Articket

Free entrance to seven big museums (Museu Nacional d'Art de Catalunya, Museu d'Art Contemporani de Barcelona, Fundació Joan Miró, Fundació Antoni Tàpies, Centre de Cultura Contemporània de Barcelona, Museu Picasso, La Pedrera Caixa Catalunya). This ticket is available at the tourist information center Plaça de Catalunya and Plaça Sant Jaume or online at www.barcelonaturisme.com. It costs 19 €/pers. and is valid for six months. www.articketbcn.org

GETTING AROUND IN BARCELONA

Local Public Transport

Transports Metropolitans de Barcelona (TMB)

www.tmb.net (CA, ES, EN)
On its website, TMB offers subway and bus maps as pdf downloads and interactive line maps.

Metro, High-Speed Railway (FGC) and Bus

There are six metro lines (subway) and FGC high-speed railway lines for public transportation connecting all parts of the city. They circulate Sun–Thu 5 am to midnight, Fri and before holidays 5 pm to 2 am, Sat non-stop service. The municipal buses circulate between 5 am and 11 pm and a night bus called Nitbús offers transportation services on the main routes from 11 pm to 5 am. The Tibibús circulates between the Plaça de Catalunya and the Tibidabo amusement park stopping also at the Park Güell. The bus only circulates during the opening hours of the park. The spacious Tombbús circulates through the shopping areas of Barcelona from the Plaça de Catalunya, down the Rambles and the Passeig de Gràcia to the Plaça Pius XII. **Tickets** are available at the vending counters and machines in the subway stations as well as from Turisme de Barcelona, the TMB customer service center at the Plaça Universitat, at the Sagrada Família and in the Estació Central de Sants. Bus tickets can be purchased directly from the bus driver. Single tickets with subway or bus start at 1.35 €, a ticket for 10 journeys is 7.70 €, a day ticket costs 5.80 €, a two-day ticket costs 10.70 € and a three-day ticket is 14.30 €.

Tramvia Blau
The nostalgic streetcar connects Plaça de Kennedy with the bottom lift station of the Tibidabo cable car. During summer, the streetcar departs every 30 mins and a one-way ticket costs 2.70 €.

Cog Railway and Cable Cars
The **Funicular de Montjuïc** starts from the Plaça Raquel Meller/Paral•lel subway station to the Av. de Miramar/Plaça Dante on the Montjuïc (in summer from Mon to Fri 7.30 am to 10 pm, Sat and Sun 10 am to 10 pm, in winter Mon to Fri 7.30 to 8 pm, Sat and Sun 9 am to 8 pm).
The cable cars of the Transbordador Aéreo start from the Torre de Sant Sebastià in Barceloneta and go up to the Montjuïc. There is a stop at the Torre de Jaume I (daily 11 am to 5.30 pm, these times vary, a single ticket costs 9 €).
The Funicular del Tibidabo connects the Plaça Dr. Andreu with the Tibidabo Amusement Park. From Jan–April and Oct–Dec, the funicular railway operates only when the amusement park is open, one-way ticket 2 €.

Cabs
Fono Taxi, Phone: +34 / 93 / 3 00 11 00
Barna Taxi, Phone: +34 / 93 / 3 57 77 55 and +34 / 93 / 3 00 23 14
Taxi Groc, Phone: +34 / 93 / 3 22 22 22
www.taxibarcelona.com
Taking a taxi in Barcelona is moderately cheap. Taxis in Barcelona are traditionally black and yellow but there is an increasing number of white taxis on the streets of Barcelona lately. A green light on the top of the taxi indicates that it is free and can be stopped by waving the hand.

Cycle Rickshaw and Bicycle Rental

Trixi
www.trixi.com
Cycle rickshaws circulate between noon and 8 pm. Prices: 6 €/15 mins, 10 €/30 mins and 18 €/60 mins.

Bicycle Rental
Al punt de trobada, Badajoz, 24
Phone: +34 / 93 / 2 25 05 85
Daily 9 am to 1.30 pm and 4.30 pm to 8 pm
Biciclot, Passeig Marítim, 33
Phone: +34 / 93 / 2 21 97 78
www.biciclot.net

FESTIVALS & EVENTS

Calvacada de Reis (Coming of the Three Kings)
5th Jan; procession from the Christopher Columbus monument to the cathedral
Carrera Ciudad de Barcelona
March; marathon (www.theproject.es)
Festival de Guitarra
Mid of March–May; series of concerts with flamenco, jazz and classical music events
Semana Santa
Eastern; religious feasts in the Holy Week including procession on Good Friday
Dia de Sant Jordi
On St George's Day, 23rd April, it is traditional to give a rose and a book to a loved one. Sales booths are installed at the Plaça Sant Jaume and other places

Primavera del Disseny/Fotográfica
Mid of April–mid of June; international biennales for design (in uneven years) and photography (in even years)

Sónar
Mid of June; it is a three-day festival for sound art, techno music, net art and multimedia. (www.sonar.es)

Nit de Sant Joan
23rd/24th June; street festival including dance and fireworks to celebrate Midsummer

Festival El Grec
July/Aug; open air theater and music events mainly in the amphitheater Grec on the Montjuïc

Festa Major de Gràcia
Middle of Aug; big summer festival of the city district Gràcia that lasts ten days

La Diada
11th Sept; catalan national holiday

Festes de la Mercè
24th Sept; festival in honor of the city's patron saint Santa Mercedes with music, acrobatics and fireworks

Festival Internacional de Jazz de Barcelona
Oct/Nov; international jazz festival lasting several weeks (Phone: +34 / 93 / 4 81 70 40 www.theproject.es)

USEFUL NOTES

Money
National currency: Euro (€)
Bank and credit cards: You can get cash with any Maestro or credit card at one of the multiple cash machines (cajero automático). These cards are also accepted in almost all hotels, restaurants and stores.

Emergency
Police/Emergency Call: Phone: 091 or 112
Fire Department: Phone: 061
Ambulance: Phone: 080
Pharmacy: Phone: 010 or 098

Police (in case of theft and accidents): Turismo Atención, Guardia Urbana de Ciutat Vella, La Rambla, 43, Phone: +34 / 93 / 3 44 13 00

Opening Hours
Banks: Mon–Fri, 8.30/9 am to 2 pm, in winter also on Sat 8.30/9 am to 1 pm. **Shops:** Mon–Fri 9/9.30 am to 1.30 pm and 4.30/5 pm to 8/8.30 pm, Sat 9/9.30 am to 2 pm. Department stores and shopping centers do not close during midday, Mon–Sat until 9/10 pm. Smaller shops also open on holidays and/or on Sun mornings. **Museums:** Often closed on Sun afternoon and Mon. **Restaurants:** Noon to 3 pm and 9 pm to 12 pm. Usually closed on Sun

Costs & Money
In comparison with other major cities, the prices are rather moderate in Barcelona. Nevertheless, you can find expensive shops and hotels all over town. Economic accommodations are to be found in youth hostels, pensions and hostels. Prices for hotels only include the actual overnight stay and not the breakfast. A double room costs 30–70 € per night in low-budget hotel and from 180 € upward in luxury hotels.

Smoking
Since 2006, smoking is prohibited in public buildings, hotels, railway stations, airports and shopping centers as well as in public transportation in all of Spain. It is also prohibited to smoke in bars and restaurants. Bigger restaurants, however, often provide a smoking area.

When to go
There is a mild and balanced climate in Barcelona all over the year. The most enjoyable travel season is from May to June and from Sept to Oct. During July and Aug the heat can become unbearable but taking

a bath in the sea is the ideal refreshment. During these months you can stay up very long and enjoy the nights sitting on the street terraces or going to festivals. The city is generally less crowded during the summer and the majority of the restaurants, museums and stores are not opened as long as usual or are completely closed. The winter is rather cool and rainy but temperatures rarely go below freezing. Going to museums or exhibitions is the suitable activity for this time of the year.

Safety

The crime rate in Barcelona is not higher than in other European major cities and common precaution measure should suffice. Thieves are active on the Rambles, in the Barri Gòtic, on the beach and in restaurants and bars. During the night it is not recommendable wandering alone through the Barri Xinés close to the harbor.

Telephone

Area Code for Barcelona: The former city code has become part of the regular nine-digit phone number in Spain and always needs to be dialed regardless from where you call.

Calling from abroad: +34 + desired phone number without 0

Calling from Barcelona: country code + area code without 0 + desired phone number

Directory Assistance: Phone: 11 822 and www.qdq.com

Public pay phones work with coins or telephone cards (tarjetas telefónicas) that can be bought in tobacco shops. Newer pay phones also accept credit cards.

Tipping

It is normal to pay a tip of about 5–10 % of the actual invoice amount in Spain. Normally you leave the tip on the table when leaving the restaurant. Also cab drivers and hotel employees are happy about an appropriate tip.

Via Augusta

Avinguda Diagonal

Avinguda de Roma

Carrer d'Aragó

Estació Central de Sants

Carrer d'Entença

Avinguda del Paral·lel

Other titles by teNeues

ISBN 978-3-8327-9309-8

ISBN 978-3-8327-9274-9

ISBN 978-3-8327-9237-4

ISBN 978-3-8327-9247-3

ISBN 978-3-8327-9234-3

ISBN 978-3-8327-9308-1

ISBN 978-3-8327-9243-5

ISBN 978-3-8327-9230-5

ISBN 978-3-8327-9248-0

Size: **15 x 19 cm**, 6 x 7½ in., 224 pp., **Flexicover**, c. 200 color photographs,
Text: English / German / French / Spanish / Italian
www.teneues.com

Other titles by teNeues

ISBN 978-3-8327-9342-5

ISBN 978-3-8327-9343-2

ISBN 978-3-8327-9296-1

ISBN 978-3-8327-9293-0

ISBN 978-3-8327-9294-7

ISBN 978-3-8327-9295-4

Interior Pages
Cool Guide New York

Size: **15 x 19 cm**, 6 x 7 ½ in., 224 pp., **Flexicover**, c. 250 color photographs,
Text: English / German / French / Spanish
www.teneues.com

There in a jiffy: Enjoy the Catalonian capital and its sights with flights from Germany in just a little over two hours.

Exuberant Barcelona

The ancient seaport on the Costa Brava is today Spain's capital of literature and music, a richly diverse city blending tradition with the highly modern. Barcelona's lifestyle is all movement, development, go-ahead. But step back a moment into the past: In 1992, Barcelona was the proud host of the Olympics and the motto of the games "faster, higher, stronger" inspired the Spanish team especially to feats of notable achievement. Striving for peak performance is second nature to Lufthansa in making travel for customers as pleasant and convenient as possible. With its connections to the Catalonian capital, Lufthansa is truly a top favourite for a medal and a place on the podium. Back in May 1959, the airline's first flight from Hamburg to Barcelona took longer than four hours. Today, Lufthansa takes you nonstop from several German cities to the Spanish metropolis on the Mediterranean in only two and a half hours.

Lufthansa flies there – several times daily and at very attractive fares. View all the details about our flights to Barcelona and others to more than 200 destinations around the world at www.lufthansa.com. There's no better way to fly.

A STAR ALLIANCE MEMBER